Praise for *The Ten Commandments*

Peter Leithart is one of the most careful and patient, but also imaginative, readers of the biblical text that I know. This meditation on the Ten Words will richly reward every Christian reader's attention.

Alan Jacobs
Baylor University,
author of *How to Think*

We hear a lot about freedom these days, but we see around us and in ourselves a terrible enslavement to human weakness, vice, political ideology, and Mammon. Peter Leithart mines the riches of the biblical tradition to show us the way to true freedom.

R. R. Reno
editor of *First Things*

Specific but not moralistic, Scripture-laden but not biblicistic, visionary but not brash—Peter Leithart's *The Ten Commandments* commands the reader's attention. Here is a treatment that looks to Jesus as the heart and soul of the Ten Words.

Hans Boersma
Nashotah House Theological Seminary,
author of *Scripture as Real Presence*

This little gem of a book is the best introduction to the Ten Commandments I have yet come across. I learned something new on almost every page. A picture may speak a thousand words, but God's "Ten Words" speak a thousand pictures of the new creation that Israel and the church are to become. Leithart makes a compelling case that God gave the Ten Commandments not to curtail or frustrate human freedom but to shape it and enable it to flourish. Every serious Christian needs to heed these Ten Words because, as Leithart explains, they're all about Jesus, God's one Word made flesh.

Kevin J. Vanhoozer
Trinity Evangelical Divinity School,
author of *Biblical Authority after Babel*

The Ten Commandments seem like an ancient relic, but Leithart shows their modern relevance. They reveal who God is and who his people are to be. Leithart shows that the Commandments are addressed to God's son. Jesus is God's faithful Son, and in Jesus we are God's faithful children. The Ten Commandments reveal Jesus. As Leithart says, "Is the Decalogue for us? We might as well ask, Is Jesus for us?"

Patrick Schreiner
Western Seminary
author of *The Kingdom of God*

THE
TEN COMMANDMENTS

THE TEN COMMANDMENTS

A Guide to the Perfect Law of Liberty

PETER J. LEITHART

LEXHAM PRESS

The Ten Commandments: A Guide to the Perfect Law of Liberty
Christian Essentials

Copyright 2020 Peter J. Leithart

Lexham Press, 1313 Commercial St., Bellingham, WA 98225
LexhamPress.com

Unless otherwise noted, Scripture quotations are from the author's own translation or are from the King James Version.

Scripture quotations in the series preface are from *ESV*® Bible (*The Holy Bible, English Standard Version*®), copyright © 2001 by Crossway Bibles, a publishing ministry of Good News Publishers. Used by permission. All rights reserved.

Scripture quotations marked (NASB) are from the New American Standard Bible®, Copyright 1960, 1962, 1963, 1968, 1971, 1972, 1973, 1975, 1977, 1995 by The Lockman Foundation. Used by permission.

Scripture quotations marked (KJV) are from the King James Version. Public domain.

Print ISBN 9781683593553
Digital ISBN 9781683593560
Library of Congress Control Number:2019951006

Lexham Editorial: Todd Hains, Jeff Reimer, Danielle Thevenaz
Cover Design: Eleazar Ruiz
Typesetting: Abigail Stocker

To Warren Gaines Leithart, son of the King:

May the God who spoke the world in ten words
forever keep you by his Spirit in
the way of Sinai's ten words.

CONTENTS

CHRISTIAN ESSENTIALS

SERIES PREFACE

T he Christian Essentials series passes down tradition that matters.

The church has often spoken paradoxically about growth in Christian faith: to grow means to stay at the beginning. The great Reformer Martin Luther exemplified this. "Although I'm indeed an old doctor," he said, "I never move on from the childish doctrine of the Ten Commandments and the Apostles' Creed and the Lord's Prayer. I still daily learn and pray them with my little Hans and my little Lena." He had just as much to learn about the Lord as his children.

The ancient church was founded on basic biblical teachings and practices like the Ten Commandments, baptism, the Apostles' Creed, the Lord's Supper, the Lord's Prayer, and corporate worship. These basics of the Christian life have sustained and nurtured every generation of the faithful—from the apostles to today. They apply equally to old and young, men and women, pastors and church members. "In Christ Jesus you are all sons of God through faith" (Gal 3:26).

We need the wisdom of the communion of saints. They broaden our perspective beyond our current culture and time. "Every age has its own outlook," C. S. Lewis wrote. "It is specially good at seeing certain truths and specially liable to make certain mistakes." By focusing on what's current, we rob ourselves of the insights and questions of those who have gone before us. On the other hand, by reading our forebears in faith, we engage ideas that otherwise might never occur to us.

The books in the Christian Essentials series open up the meaning of the foundations of our faith. These basics are unfolded afresh for today in conversation with the great tradition—grounded in and strengthened by Scripture—for the continuing growth of all the children of God.

> *Hear, O Israel: The Lord our God, the Lord is one. You shall love the Lord your God with all your heart and with all your soul and with all your might. And these words that I command you today shall be on your heart. You shall teach them diligently to your children, and shall talk of them when you sit in your house, and when you walk by the way, and when you lie down, and when you rise. You shall bind them as a sign on your hand, and they shall be as frontlets between your eyes. You shall write them on the doorposts of your house and on your gates.* (Deuteronomy 6:4–9)

AND GOD SPAKE ALL THESE WORDS, SAYING,

I am **THE LORD THY GOD**, which have brought thee out of the land of Egypt, out of the house of bondage. Thou shalt have no other gods before me.

Thou shalt not make unto thee any graven image, or any likeness of any thing that is in heaven above, or that is in the earth beneath, or that is in the water under the earth: Thou shalt not bow down thyself to them, nor serve them: for I **THE LORD THY GOD** am a jealous God.

Thou shalt not take the name of **THE LORD THY GOD** in vain; for **THE LORD** will not hold him guiltless that taketh his name in vain.

Remember the sabbath day, to keep it holy.

Six days shalt thou labor, and do all thy work:

But the seventh day is the sabbath of **THE LORD THY GOD.**

Honor thy father and thy mother: that thy days may be long upon the land which **THE LORD THY GOD** giveth thee.

Thou shalt not kill.

Thou shalt not commit adultery.

Thou shalt not steal.

Thou shalt not bear false witness against thy neighbor.

Thou shalt not covet.

INTRODUCTION

Father to Son

God spoke the Ten Commandments to Israel at Sinai. Are they for *us*? Are they for us *Christians* who are not Jews, or should Christians live by a "New Testament ethic"? Are they for us Germans or Japanese or Nigerians or Peruvians or Americans? Are they only for Israel or for the nations?

The church has always taken the Decalogue, with modifications, as God's word to Christians.[1] New Testament writers quote it, church fathers appeal to it, Thomas Aquinas comments on it, Reformation catechisms and confessions teach it, prayer books incorporate it into our worship, and church architects carve it on our walls. Christian rulers like Alfred the Great made the Decalogue the basis of civil law.

Has the church been right? Or is this an unfortunate old covenant residue that needs to be purged from the church?

Read in canonical context, the Decalogue presents itself as a Christian text. To see how, we need to examine the text carefully.

Scripture doesn't use the phrase "Ten Commandments." Exodus 20 and Deuteronomy 5 record Yahweh's "Ten *Words*" (Exod 34:28; Deut 4:13). These texts contain imperatives, but, like the rest of Torah, they include declarations, warnings, promises. That multiplicity of speech acts is better captured by the phrase "Ten Words" or "Decalogue," which I use throughout this book.

Israel has been in the wilderness for three months when they arrive at Sinai (Exod 19:1). Behind them are the ruins of Egypt, blighted by plagues. They've passed through the sea, received manna and water, grumbled and rebelled. Now the God who revealed his Name to Moses at Sinai (Exod 3:1–12) unveils himself to Israel.

God speaks on the third *day* of the month (Exod 19:16). Yahweh[2] descends with a trumpet blast that summons Israel to assembly. From a fiery cloud, he speaks the Ten Words.

He's spoken ten words before. Ten times Genesis 1 repeats, "And God spoke." At Sinai, God again speaks ten words that, if guarded and obeyed, will form Israel into a new creation. These ten new-creative words present the form of new creation.[3]

Yahweh has spoken on the third day before too. On the original third day, in the seventh of ten creation words, Yahweh called the land to bring forth grass with seed and trees with fruit (Gen 1:11). Speaking from Sinai, he reminds Israel that he brought them from the land of Egypt (Exod 20:2). Israel later commemorates Sinai at Pentecost, a feast of firstfruits. At Sinai, Israel *is* the firstfruits, a people of grain and fruit, the first to rise from the land. God speaks so that the vine brought from Egypt (Ps 80; Isa 5) will become fruitful. He speaks in anticipation of *Jesus'* third day, when the risen Lord becomes firstborn from the dead.[4]

The speaker identifies himself as "Yahweh," who is "*thy* God." At the burning bush (Exod 3), he calls himself "I am who I am." The Hebrew verbs can be translated with any tense: "I will be who I will be; I am who I will be; I will be who I was."[5] The context clarifies. Yahweh sees Israel's affliction and hears their cries. He comes to deliver from slavery. "Yahweh" is the God who will be everything Israel needs and do everything Israel needs done. Everything he is, Yahweh is *for Israel*. "Yahweh" is *Israel's* God, the God of Abraham, Isaac, and Jacob, who makes and keeps promises to his people. He is Yahweh "*thy* God."

To whom is Yahweh speaking? The answer isn't as simple as it seems. When Israel arrives at Sinai, Yahweh designates Moses as his spokesman. After the Ten Words, Moses ascends into the cloud to receive the Lord's word (20:21–22). But Moses is at the foot of Sinai when God speaks the Ten Words (19:25; 20:1). After six speeches to Moses (19:3, 9, 10, 20, 21, 24), God speaks a seventh time to all Israel (cf. 20:18). The Ten Words alone are unmediated, spoken to firstfruits sprung up from Egypt.

But there's a grammatical puzzle. Yahweh speaks to all Israel, but the verbs are in the masculine singular of the second person. The KJV gets it right: "*Thou* shalt have no other gods before me"; "*Thou* shalt not kill"; "*Thou* shalt not steal."[6] It sounds as if God is speaking to an individual man: "You, man, I brought you out of slavery. You, man, don't worship idols, kill, steal, commit adultery, or covet."

Perhaps the grammar indicates that *every* individual must obey. Perhaps God addresses Israelite *men* in particular. Men labor and rule a house, so they have authority to give rest on the Sabbath. Israelite *men* are forbidden to desire their neighbor's wife.

I think something else is going on. We may ask, *Who* was delivered from the house of bondage? Israel, of course, but Israel as *son* of Yahweh (see Exod 4:23). Yahweh's "family" tie to Israel provides a legal basis for his demand to Pharaoh: "Israel is *my* son. You have no right to enslave my son. Let my son go." When Pharaoh refuses, Yahweh cuts off negotiations and takes up the role of a kinsman redeemer, rescuing his son with a mighty hand and outstretched arm. Yahweh's justice is precise: Pharaoh seized Yahweh's firstborn; at Passover, Yahweh takes Pharaoh's.

God gave his first command to Adam, his first son.[7] At Sinai, he speaks to his son, the new Adam. The Ten Words are imperatives, but not merely imperatives. When Father Yahweh speaks to son Israel, he discloses his likes and dislikes. The Ten Words are "a personal declaration"[8] that reveals *Yahweh's* character.

Like Proverbs, they're a Father-son talk. The ten new-creative words are designed to form Israel into an image of his Father.

The Decalogue is about Israel's mission. When Israel obeys the Ten Words, his common life becomes a living, filial icon of the heavenly Father among the nations of earth. Hearing the voice from Sinai, Israel takes up Adam's vocation of imitating and imaging his Father.

Many complain about the negativity of the Ten Words. There are two positive commandments—remember the Sabbath day, honor your father and mother. Mostly, it's one "Don't" after another.[9] God says he brought Israel from slavery, but it may seem he just imposed a different slavery.

According to Scripture, Torah is the "perfect law of liberty" (Jas 1:25; 2:12). A community dominated by disrespect for parents, workaholism, violence, envy, theft, and lies isn't free. Besides, *absolute* freedom is impossible. In the world God made, the world that actually exists, things aren't free to do or be anything they please. They're free when they become what they are. An acorn is free to become an oak, not an elephant. The Ten Words guide Israel to grow up to be what he is, the son who rules in his Father's house (see Gal 4:1–7).

Israel cannot listen to the Lord's voice. He asks Yahweh to speak through Moses (Exod 20:18–21). At Sinai, the son's heart is too hardened to hear his Father. But Israel isn't left hopeless. Yahweh *will* have a son who conforms to the Ten Words. The Father *does* have such a Son, the eternal Son who became Israel to be and do what Israel failed to be and do.

The Ten Words are a character portrait of Jesus, *the* Son of God.[10] The Ten Words lay out the path of *imitatio Dei* because they lay the path of the *imitatio Christi*. As Israel kept the commandments, Augustine wrote, "the life of that people foretold and foreshadowed Christ."[11] As Irenaeus said, *Christ* fulfills the law that he spoke from Sinai.[12] The law exposes our sin, restrains the unruly, provides a guide to life. But Jesus is the heart and soul of the Decalogue. The first use of the law is the christological.

Many centuries after Sinai, God returned in the third month, in rushing wind and fire, to pour out his Spirit. At that completed Pentecost, the Spirit began to write "not on stone but on the heart" (see 2 Cor 3:3).[13] He forms a new Israel, a company of sons who share Jesus' Spirit of sonship. By that Spirit, the Father fulfills his ten new-creative words *in us*.

Is the Decalogue for us? We might as well ask, Is *Jesus* for us?

AND GOD SPAKE
ALL THESE WORDS

TWO TABLES

We know there are *Ten* Words. Yahweh wrote them with his finger on two tablets of stone (Exod 31:18; 34:1). But the church has never agreed on how to count to ten.

The Bible doesn't give a decisive answer. There are *twelve* negative imperatives in Exodus 20:1–17,[14] and one of the ten ("Honor thy father and mother") doesn't include any negatives. To make ten, Augustine combined the prohibition of images with the prohibition of idolatry and argued there were two commandments against coveting.[15] Origen separated the prohibition of false gods from the command against images and counted only one command against coveting.[16] Roman Catholics and Lutherans follow Augustine; Reformed churches follow Origen (see pages 14–15). I follow the Reformed numbering, with an Orthodox modification: Yahweh's declaration "I am Yahweh your God" is part of the First Word, not a "preface" (as in *Westminster Larger Catechism*, q. 101).[17]

To make matters more confusing, we're never told what was on each of the two stone tablets. Following Augustine, Caesarius of Arles said the first tablet contained three commandments; the second, seven.[18] Origen and others divided the commandments into four and six. Perhaps all Ten Words were on *both* tablets, a double witness to Yahweh's covenant with Israel.[19]

We can sort through some of these debates by paying close attention to the text of Exodus 20. Whatever the two tablets contained, *literally* the Ten Words aren't divided as 3 + 7 or 4 + 6, but in half, 5 + 5.[20]

Each of the first five has an explanation attached to it. Exodus 20:2 grounds the first word (v. 3): *Because* Yahweh brought Israel from Egypt, Israel should have no other gods. The next four also contain explanations: Don't bow to images, because God is jealous; don't bear the name lightly, because Yahweh punishes; keep Sabbath, because Yahweh kept Sabbath; honor father and mother to prolong your days. By contrast, none of commandments 6–10 is explained.

"Yahweh" appears eight times in the first five words (Exod 20:2–12) but isn't named at all in commandments 6–10. The style of the second half is dramatically different. In Hebrew, the first five commandments contain 145 words; the second five use only 26.[21] In Hebrew, the sixth, seventh, and eighth have only two words each: Not kill, not adultery, not steal.

Why would the Lord speak the Ten Words in two sets of five?[22]

Five is a military number (Exod 13:18, "martial array" is literally "fively"), and the Ten Words are given to Yahweh's "hosts" on their way to conquer Canaan. We have five fingers on each hand; the Ten Words are a two-handed summation of Torah. 5 + 5 patterns appear elsewhere in Scripture.[23] In the inner sanctuary of the temple was the ark of the covenant, Yahweh's throne, which contained the two tablets with their 5 + 5 words. In the Holy Place were ten lampstands arranged in two rows of five (1 Kgs 7:49) and ten tables of showbread in two rows of five (2 Chr 4:8). Outside in the courtyard, ten water stands in two rows of five formed a gauntlet, a water passage, leading to the temple door (1 Kgs 7:27–37).

The temple architecturally symbolizes the movement of the word from Yahweh's throne, through his house, out into the world. Cherubim guardians flank the ark, each with four faces: ox, lion, eagle, and man. Two cherubim match the two tablets, calling attention to the cherubic character of the law. Like the cherubim, the Ten Words guard the throne. Each cherub face reveals a facet of the law. The Torah is a threshing ox, providing bread. It's a ferocious lion that tears us, and God's enemies, to pieces. Torah offers soaring vistas like an eagle in flight and makes us truly, cherubically, human. Torah is good, but not safe. In the liturgy, you come within range of this cherubic word, a fiery sword that divides and consumes to make you a living sacrifice (cf. Heb 4:12–13).

COMMANDMENT	LUTHERAN + CATHOLIC
First	No other gods, no images
Second	Don't take Name in vain
Third	Remember Sabbath
Fourth	Honor father and mother
Fifth	Do not kill
Sixth	Do not commit adultery
Seventh	Do not steal
Eighth	Do not bear false witness
Ninth	Do not covet house
Tenth	Do not covet wife, etc.

REFORMED	ORTHODOX
No other gods	I am Yahweh; no other gods
No images	No images
Don't take Name in vain	Don't take Name in vain
Remember Sabbath	Remember Sabbath
Honor father and mother	Honor father and mother
Do not kill	Do not kill
Do not commit adultery	Do not commit adultery
Do not steal	Do not steal
Do not bear false witness	Do not bear false witness
Do not covet	Do not covet

As the 5 + 5 word proceeds from the cherub throne, it's symbolized by 5 + 5 lampstands. The law is light, illuminating hearts, lighting the community of those who hear, exposing hidden things in dark corners. Ten Words become bread on ten tables, living bread by which we live, for we do not live by bread alone but by the word that proceeds from our Father's mouth. In the Ten Words, Father Yahweh gives light and life to Israel.

Torah wasn't supposed to stay in the house. As the 5 + 5 word feeds and illumines Israel, it becomes a 5 + 5 set of water chariots, a river flowing from the sanctuary to the land and the world. Yahweh's law goes forth from Zion, to draw gentiles, to fertilize creation, until nations beat swords into plows and spears to pruning hooks (Isa 2:1–4). Torah flows out to make the world more like the sanctuary, rich with the light and bread of God.

The Bible is also full of pairs, like the twin tablets of stone. There were two cherubim in the temple (1 Kgs 6:23–28), two pillars at the temple door (1 Kgs 7:15–22), two witnesses in various narratives.[24] One relevant pair is priest and king. The first five words are priestly, focusing on the sanctuary—worship, images, Yahweh's Name, the Sabbath, and honor of parents. The second five commandments are royal, having to do with political life in the land.

Jesus sums up the entire law in a pair of commandments: Love God with all your heart, soul, strength, and mind, and your neighbor as yourself (Luke 10:27; see also Gal 5:14). As

Justin Martyr,[25] Irenaeus,[26] Augustine,[27] and many others have said, Jesus' two commandments summarize the two tables of the Decalogue. In the outline I'm using, the first five teach love for God, and the second fill out how we love our neighbor.

Each of the Ten Words addresses an arena of human life: worship, time-keeping, family, violence, sex, property, speech, desire. Yet they overlap and interpenetrate.[28] Each word implies all the others. To obey the First Word, you must also refuse images; bear God's Name; keep Sabbath; honor parents; and refrain from murder, theft, adultery, slander, greed, and lust. We keep Sabbath to honor the one God, to glorify his Name, to give life and protect property, to cultivate contentment and thankfulness. Idolatry is a kind of theft, a form of marital infidelity to the divine Husband, false witness about the living God. Every commandment is a window through which we view the whole Decalogue.

The sequence of commandments isn't arbitrary. As we'll see, Sabbath-keeping (Fourth Word) implies care of parents (Fifth). Dishonor of parents (Fifth) is a kind of murder (Sixth). Murder (Sixth) and adultery (Seventh) are intimately linked, as in the tragedy of David, Bathsheba, and Uriah.

For this same reason, one act of disobedience is infested with others. "No sin comes alone," Luther said, "but it always prompts another one after it." Lust and adultery are quickly followed by lies, "and after that comes manslaughter and bloodshed and finally despair."[29] To offend at one point is to offend in all.

Once again, we see how the Decalogue reveals Jesus, who alone lives as Yahweh's Son, keeping the whole law. He is the Word, Light, and Bread of the Father, whose Spirit flows from the temple of his body to bring life to the world.

COMMANDMENT I

I AM THE LORD THY GOD,

which have brought thee
out of the land of Egypt,
out of the house of bondage.

Thou shalt have no other gods before me.

"THOU SHALT HAVE NO OTHER GODS BEFORE ME"

On a visit to South Korea, I toured a crowded Buddhist monastery. My host told me that university placement tests were approaching and mothers were offering incense and praying for their children. I saw a woman step out of the shrine to take a cell phone call. Then she returned to her idol.

I thought of Isaiah 44: With bits of metal you make your cell phone, and with another bit you make an image and say, "Behold our God."

Idols have mouths, eyes, ears, feet, and noses, but cannot speak, see, hear, walk, or smell. Ominously, the psalmist adds, "Those who worship them shall become like them" (Ps 115). Idolatry produces "sensory organ malfunction."[30] Idols are stupid and make us stupid. They make their worshipers as dead as they are.

Ancient polytheists lived in fear. Their gods were unpredictable, liable to set traps. No one could satisfy all of them. Somewhere, one would be offended at being neglected and take his gleeful vengeance. In the exodus, Yahweh freed his son Israel from Egypt's thousands of gods (see Josh 24:14), snatching him from deadly idols. The First Word is a summons to walk in resurrection life.

The First Word infuses the Decalogue. Thomas Aquinas said that since God is the end of human life and society, worship is the first commandment.[31] According to Luther, the First Word calls us to faith, and "everything proceeds from the power of the First Commandment."[32] Every sin is betrayal, infidelity to the God who made us his own.[33] The First Word begins with a brief summary of the exodus (Exod 20:2), and that narrative snippet frames the entire Decalogue. Israel has been freed, so they are to live as a free people. They have undergone an exodus, and so are to live as an exodus people.

Literally, the First Word says, in seven Hebrew words, "There shall not be for you another god before my face." "Before my face" means "in my presence," specifically "in my presence in the sanctuary." It doesn't merely refer to ranking (no God higher than me) but to position (no God in my vicinity). Manasseh defiantly violates this commandment when he places a false god in the temple, before the face of Yahweh (2 Kgs 21:7).

Of course, Israel wasn't free to worship other gods *outside* the sanctuary. Yahweh tells Ezekiel (Ezek 14) that Israel's elders built shrines for idols in their hearts. Whenever they come before Yahweh, their idols trundle along with them. The new covenant intensifies this point. Jesus dwells in our hearts by his Spirit, who consecrates our bodies as temples (1 Cor 6). The idols of our hearts are before the face of God as blatantly as Manasseh's.

Perhaps few of you have seen idolatry in practice. None of you, I presume, has a shrine to Baal or Allah in your basement. But we're hardly free of idols. Luther wrote that the First Word requires us to "fear, love, and trust in God above all things."[34] The *Lord* is our Judge, Savior, and Lawgiver. He blesses and curses, bears our sins, speaks a trustworthy, authoritative word. When we tremble before other judges or hope in other saviors, when we pile up our sins on anyone but Jesus, idols occupy our hearts and take control.[35]

Do you fear the opinions of others? Are you paralyzed by worry about how your father or mother will evaluate you? You've set up an idol, a substitute judge—public opinion, a perfectionist father, a hypercritical mother. Have you ever thought: "If only we had a bit more money, our lives would be happy. If only I could get a better job or enjoy a flawlessly decorated home, life would be good." You're looking to a counterfeit savior—money, success, velvety comforts.

When you're cornered, do you lash out and blame others? Do you have so much trouble admitting your sins that you scapegoat your wife or husband, your parents or children? Or do you flagellate yourself for your failures or perceived failures?

You're an idolater, dumping sins on scapegoats or treating yourself as a gimcrack Jesus.

Whose imperatives do you obey? Does the voice in your head come from advertisements, popular songs, YouTube or Netflix shows? Who is your *true* Lord—not your *professed* Lord, but the one who *actually* speaks with authority into your life? If the voice in your head says "Do this," but the voice from Sinai says "Don't," which do you listen to? When you silence the Lord's voice, you've deafened yourself because there's an idol in your ears.

Idols like company. Idolatry is inherently polytheistic. Idols feed off one another, cluster together, transmogrify to keep hold of your heart. Your idols feed off the idols of others. Codependency is more biblically characterized as co-idolatry.

A husband has a drinking problem, which is an idol problem: The sanctuary of his heart is teeming with false gods. He loves a buzz more than God, and seeks a pathetic, temporary salvation in another bourbon or light beer. His bar mates become his judges, as he lives for their approval. Cornered, he pulls another idol out of storage: He rages at his wife's complaints, judging her as if he were the God of Sinai, or piling his sins on her, as if she were the Suffering Servant. Sometimes, whimpering with remorse, he puts himself on the cross. Soon, other gods come back and he's back at the bar for another round.

Meanwhile, his wife's heart is equally infested with idols. She acts out a martyr script, since she's the only one who can save the family and keep everything together. She judges her husband, finds comfort in the approval of friends, stays with her no-good husband because she's afraid of the alternative. Both are slaves. Neither will be free until they smash their co-idols to powder.

At least in *public*, we might think, our secular society has scoured the idols. That's wishful thinking. Modernity manufactures as many idols as any age. Mammon rules the market. We kill to keep ourselves comfortably surrounded by more and new stuff. "Follow your heart" replaces "Thus saith the Lord" as the unquestioned cultural imperative. Nations claim authority over our bodies and souls, demanding patriotic sacrifice on the altar of the nation. Liberal order is a conspiracy to guard public life from God's intrusions. We strip the town square, then genuflect to the nothing.

But for us, there is one God and one Lord, Jesus Christ (1 Cor 8:6). When we worship the one God, our hearts can be single, our desires focused, our lives whole. Idols tear us apart, with their contradictory, shape-shifting demands. We find coherence and integrity in keeping the First Word.

No *society* can be harmonious if everyone worships one's own god. Israel's first freedom isn't freedom to worship anything he pleases. The First Word shouldn't be confused with the First Amendment. "Thou shalt have no other gods before me" is a declaration of independence for a society free of the empty, emptying gods who compete for our love, loyalty, hope, and trust. Politics is constituted in worship, the gesture of homage before an ultimate authority. If we don't honor the living God, we'll bow before some terrible idol, who will devour our souls. A people that keeps the First Word becomes a corporate human image of the one God.

Right from the beginning, Israel prefers idols. Yahweh writes the Ten Words on stone tablets, but Moses has no sooner received them than he rushes down the mountain to shatter the golden calf. Already at Sinai, we get a preview of Israel's history of idolatry, image-worship, blasphemy, and Sabbath-breaking. Already at the foot of Sinai, we know we need God's Word written on our hearts by the finger of the Spirit. We need a mediator better than Moses, one who can demolish the idols of our hearts.

The promise of the new covenant is *not* that we're liberated from God's word, but that we're liberated to *keep* it. Jesus, the true Son, lives in utter devotion to his Father. He brings no other god before him. His obedience to the First Word gets him killed, but in his life, death, and resurrection he annihilates idols and destroys the works of the devil. God speaks to us who are sons in the Son: "Little children, guard yourselves from idols" (1 John 5:21).

In Christ, the First Word isn't a mere prohibition. It's a call to arms.[36] By it, the Lord enlists us to follow the new Joshua as he purges the planet of every vain imagination (2 Cor 10:5). Jesus has judged the world and triumphed over principalities and powers, and by the Spirit he recruits us as his hosts. The First Word creates a company of subversives who refuse to bow to the thousand-and-one idols of the age. The First Word is a call to mission and a pledge of the Lord's intention: there *will* be a day when every knee will bow, when there *will* be no other gods before him.

COMMANDMENT II

THOU SHALT NOT MAKE UNTO THEE ANY GRAVEN IMAGE,

or any likeness of any thing
that is in heaven above,
or that is in the earth beneath,
or that is in the water under the earth:
Thou shalt not bow down thyself to them,
nor serve them:

for I **THE LORD THY GOD** am a jealous God.

"THOU SHALT NOT MAKE THEE ANY GRAVEN IMAGE"

In some churches, the Second Word is tangled in debates about whether Christians may paint pictures or sculpt sculptures of Jesus or God the Father. Some believe the commandment prohibits art, especially representational art, in a place of worship. Some claim it prohibits representational art as such.

If it forbids *making* images, it prohibits *all* images. The commandment doesn't say, "Don't make images of God." It says, "Don't make graven images of things in heaven, on the earth, or in the waters under the earth." That covers *everything*, because there ain't nothing anywhere except in heaven, earth, or under the earth.

If the commandment prohibited locating images in a place of worship, it would contradict other commandments. Yahweh

33

tells Moses to "make two cherubim of gold" (Exod 25:18), a lampstand with cups "shaped like almond blossoms" (25:33), and pomegranates of blue and scarlet material (28:33). Cherubim are heavenly things, almonds and pomegranates earthly things. If the Second Word prohibits representational art, the Lord didn't stick with his program very long.

The Second Word prohibits making images for a particular purpose—to bow before and serve them. The two verbs in Exodus 20:5 are typical words for worship. "Worship" describes a bodily posture, "prostrate oneself." "Serve" is a general term for the work of Levites and priests. Ancient pagan priests serviced images of their gods. Priests brought meals to the image, cleaned it, bowed before it, praised it. That's the ministry Yahweh forbids in his house.

The commandment forbids certain liturgical *actions*. Yahweh doesn't say Israel is free to use their bodies any way they like, so long as they hold correct thoughts in their head or good feelings in their souls. Of course, bodily actions embody intentions. If a son of Aaron bent before the lampstand to pick up a piece of bread, he wouldn't violate the Second Word. Yet, God cares about what we do with our *bodies*. A good intention doesn't purify a bad action.

Did ancient people think that the image *was* the god? The answer, at least for thoughtful elites, is no. Most understood that the chunk of stone wasn't Athena; the bronze image wasn't Baal, Asherah, or Ra. Ancient priests performed rites to "quicken" divine essence in the statue. Service to the image was service to the god because the quickened image was a "sacrament" of the god's presence.

Yahweh's prohibition of images is more radical than we realize. He's not merely saying, as Clement of Alexandria thought, that we shouldn't confer power on things we make.[37] He isn't saying, "I'm not made of stone, wood, bronze, gold." Everyone *knew* that. He's saying, "Don't think you can serve me by serving an image, or honor me by honoring a likeness." Yahweh's priests served him and cared for his house, but what occupied the house was the living Lord himself, Yahweh's glorious personal *Name* (1 Kgs 3:2; 5:3–5; 8:16–18).

In the judgment of my Reformed Protestant tradition, some churches today are corrupted by the idolatry condemned by the Second Word. No Christian believes an icon is identical to the saint. No one thinks an icon of Christ *is* Christ. Yet some Christians treat icons as "sacraments" of Christ and his saints; they venerate the icon as homage to the one pictured. That's exactly what the Second Word forbids.

Above I used the word "sacrament." Christians *do* have physical signs of God's presence, the water of baptism and the bread and wine of the Eucharist. We know we commune with the body and blood of Jesus because the Lord *promised* to meet us at the table (1 Cor 10:16–17). He hasn't promised to encounter us through pictures. When Christians seek Jesus through an image, they're looking for God in the wrong place.

Honoring God in images isn't just fruitless. It arouses the jealousy of Yahweh. In Scripture, jealousy expresses spurned love. Yahweh addresses Israel as "son," but "jealous" opens a marital perspective on their relationship. Husbands claim their wives' affection, and wives are rightly jealous of their husband's attention. As Origen noted, Yahweh speaks as a jealous bride groom to warn his bride to flee fornication.[38] Bowing to and serving images is spiritual adultery.[39]

Whatever their intentions, those who serve images "hate" Yahweh (Exod 20:5). Imagine a husband who speaks to dig ital photos of his wife, fawns on them, kisses them, gazes at them, but never notices his wife. He might say, "I demonstrate my love for my wife *by* loving her picture." But no wife would accept that evasion.

The Second Word implies a contrast between sight and hearing, eye and ear. In Deuteronomy 4, Moses reminds Israel they didn't see any form on Sinai, but heard a voice. When Yahweh tells Moses to carve new tablets, he uses the verb form of "graven image" (Exod 34:1): Moses "graves" tablets. But these graven stones contain *words*, not pictures. Yahweh declares commands, writes on the tablets. At Sinai, he does *not* show himself. Yahweh is the unseen God who speaks. He is Word.

Eyes are organs of scrutiny and judgment (see Ps 11:4). God sees and judges the creation good (Gen 1:31), Eve sees and evaluates the tree (Gen 3:6), Adam and Eve's eyes are opened after they eat (Gen 3:7). With visible things, we assume a stance of criticism, command, and control. But God is not under our control. We don't judge him, but he us.

Hearing has a different phenomenology. In Scripture, hearing is virtually identical to obedience.[41] To hear is to *receive* commands. Listening puts us in the position of being judged. Hearing opens an uncontrollable future: someone says, for the first time, "I love you," and the world shifts beneath your feet.

Since Sinai, God *has* been seen: The Word tabernacled in flesh and we *saw* his glory (John 1:14). Seeing Jesus, we see the Father (John 14:9). Some Christians say that Jesus' advent changes the Second Word, so that we are now permitted to serve images. But Jesus ascended and is no longer visibly present. We *don't* see his glory as the apostles did. He's with us by his Spirit, the wind who blows where he will, the Spirit whom we hear but cannot see. That Spirit comes to us in sensible forms—in audible words, tangible water, and edible food and drink. Someday we will see Jesus face-to-face. But not yet. To live by the eye is to reach ahead of our time. It immanentizes the eschaton. After the incarnation, we *still* live by ear (2 Cor 5:7), until he comes again.

The twenty-first century is an age of spectacle.[42] Every inch of wall space is filled with flickering screens. Ads entice us with dreams of the good life. A single web image sparks weeks of savage public debate, and leaders lead by projecting an image of power or relatability. Our relations to one another are no longer tangible, mediated through touch, but abstractedly visible, mediated through screens. We create technological miracles and call them tools, then adjust our lives in obedience to their requirements, panting like Pavlov's dog every time we hear a text notification ding. Who's really in charge? The Second Word summons us to resist the temptation to fear, trust, serve, and live by the spectacle. To walk faithfully, we must tune our *ears* to the Word of God.

Some use the Second Word against the Bible. Scripture describes God in human terms, as King, Lord, Husband, Shepherd, Workman, Friend. He's compared to inanimate things: Rock, Sun, Shield. If we're forbidden sculpt or paint images, some philosophers have argued, we should reject the verbal images of Scripture.[43]

That misses the Bible's primary alternative to image veneration. God prohibits veneration of graven images because he's already made his image. The creation account (Gen 1) resembles a temple construction. An ancient temple builder formed the shell, filled it with tools and furnishings, and then, at the climax, placed an image in the inner sanctuary, a sign of the god's presence and his claim on the land. Just so, Yahweh divides earth into three zones, then fills it with plants, heavenly bodies, fish and birds, land animals. The three-story universe is a cosmic temple, with every creatures designed to participate in a cosmic liturgy.

When everything is in place, Yahweh deliberates: "Let us make man in our image, according to our likeness" (Gen 1:26–28). Yahweh works the ground like a potter, forms Adam, and breathes into his nostrils the breath of life (Gen 2:7). Like an image in an ancient temple, Adam and Eve mediate the

Creator's presence and lordship. As they fill and subdue the earth, they symbolize Yahweh and his claim on the whole creation. *We* are images of God. When we venerate images, we're not merely exchanging the glory of God for the glory of creation. We give up our own glory. We're alienated from our own vocation.

Idolatry leads to injustice, oppression, the shedding of innocent blood. It's *inherently* dehumanizing because it substitutes senseless wood or stone or metal for *living* images. We keep the Second Word when we keep Jesus' second great commandment, when we do homage to God's image in our brothers and sisters, when we love and serve God in serving and loving our neighbors, when we perform the sacrifices of giving alms, doing good, sharing, and hospitality.

Aroused to jealousy, Yahweh threatens to curse idolaters to the third and fourth generation. Though attached to the Second Word, Luther is right that these words "relate to all the commandments" as a reminder that God is not to be toyed with. He "will not leave it unavenged if men turn from Him." This appendix, Luther says, is a hoop in a wreath that joins the end of the Ten Words to the beginning.[40]

It's a fearful warning, but we shouldn't miss the mercy. Early in the history of the northern kingdom of Israel, Jeroboam I sets up golden calves, violating the Second Word (1 Kgs 12:26–30). All the kings of Israel follow the sin of Jeroboam, but Yahweh arrests each dynasty after three of four generations. He doesn't let liturgical idolatry go on forever.

Besides, Yahweh isn't only a judge of sinners. He also displays his loyal love to those who love and obey him. The love lasts much, much longer than the judgment. He curses to three or four generations but shows love to thousands of generations.

COMMANDMENT III

THOU SHALT NOT TAKE
THE NAME OF THE LORD THY GOD
IN VAIN;

for **THE LORD** will not hold him
guiltless that taketh his name in vain.

"THOU SHALT NOT TAKE THE NAME OF THE LORD THY GOD IN VAIN"

What's in a name?

A name is an identifying label. This is Alex, that's Alex Jr.; this is Natalia, that's Peter. Names allow us to address one another. When you see your friend across the street, you call his name to get his attention. At a first meeting, you reveal your name, which gives the new acquaintance power to invoke you. Now he can call you from across the street.

Names are self-revealing. I say "Leithart," and many recognize my German ancestry. My mother named me for Peter Marshall, the twentieth-century Presbyterian chaplain of the US Senate. My name summarizes a family and personal history. Nicknames reveal character traits. "Slim" is obese, "Worm" reads a lot of books, "Springshanks" can dunk a basketball.

The ancient world teemed with gods. You wouldn't ask, "Do you worship God?" You'd ask, "*Which* god do you worship?" The name Yahweh distinguished the God of Israel from other gods. Yahweh isn't "God-in-general." He's "Yahweh Israel's-God."[44] By revealing his Name, Yahweh gave Israel the power to call him. Israel the son called to the heavens "Yahweh, hear us," and Father Yahweh answered.

Like human names, Yahweh's Name has to be revealed, and it is self-revealing. As Origen said, the Name is "the personal character of God."[45] On the mountain, Yahweh calls himself "Yahweh, Yahweh! Gracious and compassionate, slow to anger and abounding in loyal love, yet he by no means clears the guilty" (Exod 34:6–7). Yahweh is the God of compassion and justice, the patient God who won't let us defy him forever. Like human names, "Yahweh" summarizes a history. At the burning bush, Yahweh names himself as the God of Abraham, Isaac, and Jacob, the God who made promises to the fathers and now comes to keep his promises.[46] The Ten Words open with a story: "I am Yahweh your God, who brought you up from the land of Egypt, out of the house of slavery."

*Un*like human beings, Yahweh identifies and names *himself*. Moses asks, "What shall I say when Israel asks who sent me?" (Exod 3:13–14). Yahweh doesn't leave him guessing but unveils a Name that Moses couldn't have known otherwise. By contrast, we are *given* names. Surnames come from our parents, their parents before them, and their parents on back to the first someone who received the name. We *receive* our names and identities from others, as a gift. Yahweh, who names himself, shares that Name with Israel. The Ten Words address Israel as Yahweh's redeemed son (Exod 4:23). The Third Word assumes that family connection. As son, Israel has received the family name of Yahweh.

The Third Word is usually translated as, "Do not take the name of the Lord your God in vain," with "take" understood as "speak." Many Christians think the Third Word forbids cussing or oaths. True, the Third Word *does* require us to tell the truth (Exod 23:13; Deut 6:13).[47] When we swear in God's Name, we call him as a witness to the truth of what we're saying. Oaths are self-cursing. Taking an oath, we put ourselves on the line: "If what I say is not true, then may the Lord's curse fall on me." We take the Name of the Lord in vain when we invoke God as witness for false statements. We take his Name lightly when we call down curses without genuine fear of the Lord's judgment. The Lord forbids us to speak as if he doesn't matter.[48] Every word we speak will be brought to judgment (Matt 12:36).

The Hebrew verb, however, isn't "take" or "speak," but "lift up," "carry," or "bear." We bear God's Name on our tongues when we swear, but the Name is also imprinted on our head, hands, and feet. We bear the Name lightly with indifferent or disobedient worship (Exod 20:22–26), with casual sex (Amos 2:7), or when we steal (Lev 6:2–5).[49] Speaking or silent, active or passive, we bear the name *all* the time in *everything* we do.[50] Every sin is a violation of the Lord's holy Name, the Name he shares with us. Do we feel the weight of the Name? Or do we treat it as empty breath? Reducing the Third Word to a command about oaths turns it into a mechanism to preserve social order.[51] That misses the key demand, to honor God's Name. If we give God's Name weight, we might well become abrasive to the social status quo.

In the new covenant, we bear the Name because we're baptized into the Name of Father, Son, and Holy Spirit. With that gifted name comes a new identity, a new history, and membership in a new family. Every Sunday, this Name is re-placed on us, when the minister pronounces the benediction. Aaron "set" the Name of Yahweh on the people by blessing in the Name (Num 6:24–26). When a minister pronounces a triune blessing, the congregation assumes again its baptismal name and is commissioned once again to "bear" the name into the world. The Third Word, like the first two, is a call to mission.

Each age of Israel's history is marked by a characteristic sin, which corresponds to the first three of the Ten Words. During the period of the judges, Israel was tempted to worship the gods of the nations, a sin against the First Word. During the monarchy, Israel broke the Second Word by worshiping Yahweh at high places and through images of golden calves.

During the exile, Israel was scattered among gentiles. They no longer worshiped other gods or erected golden calves. They were called to bear the Name in the midst of the nations and were tempted to compromise and hypocrisy. By the time of Jesus, it was clear that Israel had failed. The Jewish leaders claimed to be children of Abraham, but many were children of the devil, as Jesus said (John 8:44). Jesus condemned the Pharisees and scribes as "hypocrites" who play-acted righteousness. They didn't fill out the robes they wore, nor live up to the family name (Matt 23). Because Israel didn't bear the Name weightily, they "profaned" the Name among the nations (Rom 2:24). Instead of leading gentiles to praise, they sowed blasphemy.

"Name" is a title of the Second Person of the Trinity, the Son. The Father's Name is the Son. The Father is Father only because he has a Son; his reputation is bound up with the Son; he discloses himself in the Son. During the old covenant, the Name dwelt in the temple, sanctifying the temple by his presence. Because the Name dwelt in the house, Israel had to keep the house clean. Sins had to be scoured away, the priests had to maintain the cycle of offerings, trim the lamps on the lampstand, change the showbread on the table. If Israel and the priests failed to maintain the house, it would become polluted and the Name profaned.

As the living Name, Jesus bears the full weight of the Father's Name, bears it until it crushes him and renders him nameless. He suffers our indifference and hypocrisy all the way to the cross, and so the Father raises him and gives him a Name above every Name, that at the Name of Jesus all knees should bow. The living Name goes silent, so that the nations would one day proclaim the Name of the Lord.[52] As Rabanus Maurus and others saw, the greatest sin against the Third Word is denying the Name of Jesus.[53]

Each Israelite was a house, named by the Name, and so each had to maintain the purity of the temple of their body. In the new covenant too, we're named by the Name of the Trinity and indwelt by the Spirit, who consecrates us as his sanctuary. God binds his Name and reputation to us. Whether his name is praised or blasphemed depends on whether we bear his name with the weight it deserves. It is a weighty responsibility to bear the weighty Name of the living God before the world.

COMMANDMENT IV

REMEMBER THE SABBATH DAY,

to keep it holy.

Six days shalt thou labor,

and do all thy work:

But the seventh day is the sabbath

of **THE LORD THY GOD.**

"REMEMBER THE SABBATH DAY"

Most of the Ten Words are negations: Do not, do not, do not. The prohibited behaviors are like chunks the sculptor chips away to uncover the image of *The Thinker* lurking in the marble. At the center are two positive commandments: "Remember the Sabbath" and "Honor your father and mother." When idolatry and hypocrisy have been eliminated, when violence and infidelity and theft and lies have been chiseled off, *this* is what's left: a day of joy, and harmony among generations. *This* is the gem we discover when the mud is washed away, the beauty at the heart of the new-creative "Do nots." *This* is the life God's son lives before his Father: Israel rejoicing with sons and daughters in the God who "himself is festival."[54]

The Sabbath command is perhaps the most repeated, most expanded-on, and most controverted commandment

(Exod 31:12–17; 35:1–3).[55] Sabbaths appear in instructions about other feasts (Exod 12:16; Lev 16:31), and the liturgical calendar of Leviticus 23 is organized around Sabbaths and sabbatical periods. The pattern of 6 + 1 is extended to slavery and manumission (Exod 21:1–11) and care of the land (Exod 23:10–13). Every half century, Israel was to mark Jubilee, an extended super-Sabbath (Lev 25). Sabbath was a perpetual covenant (Exod 31:16), a "sign" between Yahweh and his people (Exod 31:13, 17).

Paul includes the Sabbath among old covenant ordinances that have passed away, fulfilled in Christ (Col 2:16). Augustine,[56] Caesarius of Arles,[57] and others consider Israel's Sabbath as a type of the Christian's spiritual rest, while Augustine[58] and Bede[59] saw it also as an anticipation of eternal rest. These writers are correct that the command requires more than abstinence from work. Christians live continuously in Christ's Sabbath.[60]

Yet most Christians have seen continuing practical relevance in the Fourth Word. Early on, the church began to assemble on the first (eighth) day of resurrection. Some Christian traditions practice a full-day rest, and all traditions recognize the necessity of scheduled time for worship and the wisdom of a rhythm of labor and rest. If we spiritualize Sabbath too quickly or thoroughly, we miss its breadth. The Fourth Word teaches us how to *live*, what we do and don't do.

It begins: "Memorialize the day of ceasing." "Memorialize" is linked to the sign-character of Sabbath. The Bible's first "sign" is the rainbow. When *Yahweh* sees the bow, he "remembers" and keeps covenant (Gen 9:12–17). Similarly, Israel doesn't keep Sabbath merely by recalling it to mind. Israel does something—nothing—on Sabbath to memorialize creation, as an enacted "reminder" to Yahweh to bring creation to fulfillment in a final Sabbath.

Israel memorializes the day by ceasing (*shabat*). Work is good. Human dominion over the world is good. But God requires that we "interrupt" our work to acknowledge him as Lord,[61] as a public confession that our authority over creation is a *derived* authority.[62] Sabbath pauses life's noise. It's the silence that tunes our ears to Yahweh's word.

This dimension of the Sabbath is highlighted in the first instance of human Sabbath-keeping (Exod 16). Israel collects manna for six days but refrains on the seventh, when they trust God's provision. When Israel enters the land, manna ceases, but Israel still keeps Sabbath. Bread from earth, as much as angel bread from heaven, is a gift of God, not a sheer product of human labor. Sabbath serves as a weekly recognition of human limitations and God's generosity. Sabbath is our fundamental stance as creatures, one of receptivity.

Israel's consecration of the day depends on Yahweh's prior consecration (Exod 20:11). But the verb "keep holy" means "sanctify" or "*make* holy." Israel doesn't merely maintain the holiness of a day that is already holy. Ceasing *consecrates* the day of ceasing.

We may clarify the notion of holy time by analogy with holy space. Holy space is space God claims by being present in glory (cf. Exod 29:43). Everything associated with that space is his—people, altars, lampstands, knives, forks, snuffers. Holy things must be used solely for God's purposes. A holy fork can't be used at a barbeque. A priest can't borrow a pinch of holy incense to perfume his home.

Holy time is time claimed by God. The Sabbath is *God's* day as the tabernacle is God's space. On the Sabbath, Israel is on the *Lord's* time. If they use Yahweh's time for their own projects, they commit sacrilege and trespass a holy boundary. We're always on the Lord's time, but the Sabbath embeds that truth in weekly habit.

Israel consecrates the day by worship. At the sanctuary, priests offered extra offerings (Num 28) and throughout Israel the people gathered in local "synagogues" for praise, study of Torah, and prayer. Israel consecrated the day by gathering in the presence of the Sabbath-keeping God (Lev 23:3).

Israel also mimics Yahweh by mimicking Yahweh's *gift* of rest: Yahweh brings Israel from restless slavery; therefore, Israel gives rest to slaves. Most of Exodus 20:10 is a list of seven (!) categories of people who are *granted* rest. Each Israelite takes rest, and each also gives rest. Like Father, like son.

The Sabbath is unparalleled in the ancient world.[63] It spreads out from the seventh day to fill the nooks and crannies of Israel's life. Indentured servants are held for six years, released in the seventh. Debt isn't allowed to become a permanent burden.[64] Land could be sold for fifty years (7 Sabbath years + 1), but reverted to the original owners at Jubilee (Lev 25). At the center of the calendar in Leviticus 23, the Lord reminds Israel to care for the needy (23:22). Torah calls Israel to justice, mercy, and faithfulness, a Sabbath way of life (Isa 58). From this, it's clear that Jesus never broke Sabbath, or made exceptions. Jesus *keeps* Sabbath by giving relief to the distressed. Pulling an ox from a ditch isn't an exception to Sabbath rules (Luke 14:5). It *fulfills* Sabbath by giving rest to a suffering ox.

For these reasons, Joseph Ratzinger calls the Sabbath "the heart of all social legislation." It anticipates "the society free of domination, a foretaste of the city to come" and "the freedom of all the children of God and creation's release from anxiety."[65] In our society, leisure is a monopoly of the rich, while the poor have to work multiple jobs to eke out a subsistence living.[66] Sabbath redistributes and equalizes rest. It treats slaves as persons, not machines. It guards Israel from organizing his time for 24/7 productivity, and so defies the reign of Mammon. As Stanley Hauerwas and William Willimon put it, it's countercultural: one day each week, Christians simply refuse to show up.[67]

Sabbatical sociology is grounded in Sabbatical theology. Sabbath is Yahweh's day of joy, when he delighted in the completed creation.[68] It's socially revolutionary because it's the *Lord's* day, a holy day of worship that opens earthly time to the rhythms of heaven. All Israel, including slaves and animals, mimics the rest of God. We might expect the opposite: because it's *Yahweh's* day of ceasing, human beings *can't* cease. In ancient myths, gods make human beings to serve their divine leisure.

The Sabbath, by contrast, is premised on an analogy between God's work and human work: the Creator is himself a craftsman and a manual laborer. The Sabbath highlights an analogy between divine and human rest.

"Analogy" and "mimic" are too weak. By ceasing, son Israel *shares* his Father's Sabbatical. For Israel, this is sheer gift. Yahweh stops working because he's finished (Gen 2:1–4). Israel *hasn't* finished, and neither have we. After rest, we go back to work, but we work with the Sabbath satisfaction of a job done. By keeping Sabbath, we express confidence that the Lord will bring his work to completion and give *us* time to finish. Sharing Sabbath, we participate *already* in the divine pleasure of bringing things to an end, long before things come to their end. We enjoy now what Thomas Aquinas calls "all future blessings."[69] The Lord opens up his day of ceasing to include us, so that we *share* in his rest, like Father, like son.

Yahweh's rest is royal. After battling Pharaoh, the Divine Warrior enjoys victory. Having trampled grapes, he mixes a cup of wine. King Yahweh delivers Israel from deadly service in Pharaoh's house and brings them to Sabbath at Sinai. And so Sabbath theology circles back to Sabbath sociology. By extending Sabbath to Israel and to us, Yahweh raises his son to kingship. We work, but aren't slaves to work. We sit now in heavenly places (Eph 2:6), sharing Jesus' lordship over all. Enthroned in Sabbath glory, we with Israel participate in our Father's rest, and his rest-giving.[70]

HONOR THY FATHER AND THY MOTHER:

that thy days may be long
upon the land which
THE LORD THY GOD giveth thee.

"HONOR THY FATHER AND THY MOTHER"

The Fifth Word—"Honor thy father and thy mother"—seems stuffily conservative. In our topsy-turvy times, it's countercultural.

We late moderns confess the (authoritative?) 1960s creed, "Question authority," applied in the first instance to the family. "Don't trust anyone over thirty," until you cross that threshold yourself. Scripture doesn't treat parental authority as absolute. In some circumstances, parents must be disobeyed.[71] Yet in the Bible, authority is good, and parental authority is the original form of authority.

We believe in equality. We don't defer to our betters because we find it offensive to think we have betters. "Honor," by contrast, indicates a hierarchy. Some *deserve* more attention and respect.

We believe in the self-made man, the buffered self, the isolated individual. Every man is an Adam who has molded himself from the dust, embarrassed by the belly button that bespeaks dependence. Choice is the foundation of all moral action. Nearly any act is sanctified by "consent," the magic word of liberal order. The Fifth Word explodes satanic myths of self-creation by teaching that *un*chosen relationships have moral weight. Christians have long recognized that this principle extends beyond the family.[72] I didn't choose to be born an American or baptized as an infant, yet I should submit to the authority of these given communities.[73]

Today's families are assembled from the blistered shards of broken households. Children are "yours, mine, ours," and grow up with multiple fathers and stepfathers, mothers and stepmothers, a father and a father, a mother and a mother. While most of America's children live with two parents, a quarter of them do not. In some communities, the situation is worse: three-quarters of African American children are born outside marriage. The Fifth Word requires honor of father and mother, *both* in the *singular*, assuming that children have one of each sex as parents, both present.[74]

The Fifth Word assumes that parenthood is inescapable, but our reproductive technologies have eroded that assumption. A couple can have a genetically related child who isn't carried by the mother. Children can be manufactured from donated eggs and sperm and borne by a surrogate, so they have *no* physical connection to parents. Family is detached from biology.

Children in same-sex families *can't* be biologically related to both parents. The relationship between parents and children is legal rather than biological. Adoption is a gift to many children and families, but adoption is necessary because of death or family breakdown. Today, changes in marriage law effectively make adoption the legal paradigm for all parent-child relations. Among other things, this extends the reach of the state, as it takes oversight of all familial relations.

Christians shouldn't be seduced by nostalgia for families of the Victorian age or the 1950s. We live in our age, not theirs. Scripture, not some historical epoch, is our standard. Still, the Fifth Word has an implicit model of family and society. To keep this commandment fully, we must reconstruct the social situation it assumes—two-parent families as a norm, the goodness of authority, the limitations of consent, the preservation of families through a lifelong commitment of a man and a woman.

For Christians, the family's role is limited by the reality of the church. Churches baptize infants to mark them as children of the heavenly Father, nurtured by mother church. In the church, we have multiple fathers and mothers, sisters and brothers (Mark 10:30). Blood relations aren't erased. Peter and Andrew, John and James, were sibling-apostles, and Paul issues commands to fathers and their biological or adopted children (Eph 6:1–4). Yet the church is the Christian's primary brotherhood, our first family and a site of pedagogy and parenting. Due to revolutionary social changes, today's church has a huge mission opportunity. As one of the ten new-creative words from

Sinai, the Fifth Word forms a familial counterculture within the family of God, where broken homes can be put back together.

The Hebrew word for "honor" means "glorify," which Scripture uses to speak of honoring God. Your parents aren't God, but they're God's gifts to you, as you are God's gifts to them. The way you treat them should resemble the way you respond to God. As Karl Barth writes, God alone is literally Father because he alone gives life. But he has graciously arranged the world to permit human fatherhood and motherhood. The dignity of parents lies in their capacity to symbolize the heavenly Father.[75]

We can fill out the practical import of this commandment by asking, How do we honor God?

By praising him. Do you speak well of your parents, or do you criticize, grumble, and pretend you know better?

By serving him. The Bible tells us to rise before the hoary head (Lev 19:32). Out of respect for the old, and especially for parents, we adopt a posture of service, like a priest who stands and serves Father Yahweh.

By listening to him. The Hebrew word "glorify" comes from the word "weight." To honor parents is to give weight to their opinions, presence, advice. Whose words weigh more—your parents' or your Instagram friends? Whose voice do you listen to? Parents are called to guide children into mature wisdom. Children honor them when they acknowledge their parents have wisdom they lack, when they allow themselves to be led in the way that leads to life.[76] Children honor parents when they facilitate, rather than inhibit, their parents' mission. The Fifth is the first commandment with a promise (Eph 6:2), and the promise is inherent in the command: as parents fulfill their mission and children respect them, the children are directed toward a long life of blessing in the land.

By trusting him. We trust God to provide for us, do good, have our best interests in view. Children honor their parents by assuming that their rules and curfews and chores are intended to bless them, even if they can't see how. Children honor parents when they ask for what they need and receive what their parents give with thanks.

By submitting to discipline. God proves our sonship by disciplining us (Heb 12). When we resist God's discipline, we're not honoring him. When children fume resentfully about correction, they're disobeying the Fifth Word.

We obey the Fifth Word differently at different stages of life, but the Fifth Word is never superseded. Adult children also must honor parents—praise them, give weight to their words, trust them.

In fact, the commandment is *primarily* addressed to adult children.[77] It requires children to honor parents practically, by caring for them in old age. From this angle, we see how the Fifth Word is intertwined with the biblical vision of a just society. Honoring parents is linked to care of vulnerable orphans and widows (Ezek 22:6–8). Leviticus 19:3 commands: "You shall revere your mother and father,[78] and you shall keep my Sabbaths."[79] Reverence for mother and father, expressed in material support in old age, is a form of Sabbath-keeping. First-century Pharisees avoided this responsibility by vowing money to the temple instead of helping their parents (Mark 7:9–13). Jesus saw through the ruse and condemned them for invalidating the command of God. In Israel, abuse or neglect of parents was a public concern and punished severely.[80]

By my reckoning (see chapter 2), the Fifth Word is in the first table, connected to commandments concerning worship. Addressed to Yahweh's son Israel, the new Adam, "Honor your father" means "Honor Yahweh your Father, who brought you out of the land of Egypt."[81]

Because the Fifth Word is the heavenly Father's word to his son, it's ultimately about the Father and his eternal Son, who lives as the true Israel to redeem Israel. The Fifth Word not only assumes a certain order in society. It unveils the inner life of God. The Son honors his Father, trusts his Father, submits to his Father, hears his Father, gives the words of his Father weight, submits to his Father's discipline. But this isn't the end of the story. In the same moment, the Father turns the tables to glorify the Son, honor him, listen to his prayers and pleas.

That is the final truth of family life: Young children glorify parents, while parents raise their children to glory. Adult children honor their parents materially, while parents praise their children. In keeping the Fifth Word, family life comes to reflect the mutual honor that is the crenulated communion of the living God.

THOU SHALT NOT KILL.

"THOU SHALT NOT KILL"

Jesus summarizes the law with two commandments (Luke 10:27): Love God with all our heart, soul, strength, and mind; and love our neighbor as ourselves. These commands summarize the Ten Words: the first five commandments are about love for God, and the second five describe love for neighbor.

The sixth commandment is a suitable heading to the second half of the Decalogue. The Ten Words don't offer any rationale for prohibiting murder because the rationale is given earlier, after the flood (Gen 9:3-7). Yahweh prohibits eating blood and warns against shedding human blood:

> Whoever sheds man's blood,
> by man his blood shall be shed,
> for *in the image of God*
> *He made man.* (Gen 9:6 NASB)

Human life must be protected because human beings are made in the image of God.[82] The first commandment prohibits worship of any but the God of exodus; the first word of the second table prohibits assaults on the *created* image of that God.

The first and second halves of the Decalogue match one another: idolatry is a species of murder, murder a kind of idolatry (first and sixth); worshiping images is spiritual adultery (second and seventh); bearing God's name lightly steals his glory (third and eighth); the Sabbath is for renewing covenant vows (fourth and ninth); coveting undermines hierarchies necessary for healthy family, social, and political life (fifth and tenth).[83]

With the Sixth Word, we move from Genesis 3 to Genesis 4. Adam's original sin was idolatry, ignoring God's word (Gen 3). Eve was tempted by the devil, a murderer from the beginning (John 8:44). One of Adam's sons became a satanic murderer himself (Gen 4). The Ten Words forbid both the idolatry of Adam and the fratricide of Cain.

Each of the last five commandments is an extension of the prohibition of murder: Do not assault the image of God by killing another human being. Do not assault the image of God by violating marriage, by seizing another's property, or by defiling his reputation. When we covet, we desire and do not have, and that makes us Cains, envious murderers who attack God through his image.

English translations sometimes translate the Hebrew verb as "murder." That's too specific. The Hebrew verb is used frequently in Numbers 35, which establishes cities where man-slayers find refuge from the avenger of blood. The verb often means "murder," the intentional or premeditated killing of a man or woman (Num 35:16, 17, 18, 19, 21, 25, 26, 27). But the same verb describes what we call "manslaughter," unintentional killing or a crime of passion (Num 35:27; cf. Deut 4:42). Even the just vengeance of the avenger, a form of capital punishment, is rendered with the same verb (Num 35:27; cf. 35:30). Though the word often means "murder," its basic meaning is "manslaying."[84]

Scripture treats different sorts of killing differently. Scripture requires care for animals, but never prohibits killing animals for food. The Lord authorizes civil rulers to execute criminals (Rom 13). Scripture treats the death penalty as just, especially in cases of murder (Exod 21:23; Num 35). As Augustine said, "He does not kill who is the executor of a just command."[85] War is permissible in some circumstances (Deut 20),[86] and Israelites were permitted to kill, under restricted conditions, to defend their homes (Exod 22:2–4).

All shedding of human blood had to be dealt with, either by the confinement of the manslayer, the execution of the murderer, or a rite of cleansing (cf. Deut 21:1–9). Before soldiers went to war, they paid "atonement" money to pre-cover bloodshed (Exod 30:11–16). William Cavanaugh makes the point with provocative sharpness: we moderns gladly kill at the state's behest, but the Bible insists that we may kill *only* in the name of God.[87]

Here we can discern another "perichoretic" connection between the first and the sixth commandment. God determines when killing is permitted because of who he is: Lord of life and death. If we kill at *another's* command, that other has effectively become our God, our Lord of life and death.[88]

You might be feeling some relief right about now. At least here is *one* commandment you've never broken, not *really*, not in any serious way.

Don't let yourself off so easily. If you live in a modern society, you're entrenched in networks of violence. Entertainments thrill us through granular depictions of violence. Scripture calls false witnesses "witnesses of violence." Spend a few minutes on Twitter, and you'll see verbal mayhem. Liberal order presumes that we'll forever disagree about fundamental truths, and thus relies on good violence to counter bad. American greed for more oil, more comforts, more *stuff* drives a foreign policy of perpetual war.[89] Soldiers kill for "a state whose *very ideal* is the separation of violence from the will of God."[90]

Even Christians are happy to separate violence from the will of God. Many Christian soldiers go to war at the command of secular states, without consulting their pastors or considering whether the war is just in the Lord's sight. Few Christians think the church has any authority over a Christian's decision to fight. If God is Lord of life and death, Christians should kill only if he permits it.

Because we don't honor the family as the context for reproduction, because we demand the perfect baby or a right to a child, we've developed technologies of reproduction that create and discard embryos by the thousands. Our disobedience to the Fifth Word feeds a high-tech culture of death, buttressed by legal guarantees.[91] In most "advanced" societies, the murder of unborn babies has been industrialized. Abortion isn't a side issue. As Robert Jenson says, a key mark of civilized society is "the replacement of vendetta by courts and their officers." Legal abortion grants "the most interested party" a license to kill, a privatization of murder that is nothing less than "a relapse to pure barbarism."[92]

We can go deeper by reminding ourselves that the Ten Words are a portrait of the true Israel, the last Adam, the eternal Son, Jesus. Once we get Jesus in view, two things come clear.

First, the *teaching* of Jesus. Addressing the Sixth Word in the Sermon on the Mount, Jesus warns against hatred, anger, and angry words (Matt 5:21–26, 38–48). As Luther put it, the Sixth Word requires a pure heart as well as pure hands, since we can kill with any part of our bodies.[93] Anger can dominate one's life, churning beneath the surface and breaking through at the slightest provocation—a child's embarrassing accident, pressure at work, a traffic jam. You say you're ambitious, but what looks like ambition is envy, a desire to take down the competition. Deep down, you're a murderer. You say you're plain-speaking, but in reality you've turned your tongue into a sword that kills with insults, curses, and frothy outrage. You say you're a leader, but in fact your simmering anger intimidates everyone around you. Anger curves inward into self-hatred, cleverly disguising itself as humility.

We perfect techniques to keep anger under wraps, polish a surface of smooth sociality, most of the time. We even hide our anger from ourselves. The angriest people would be shocked to hear that they're angry, even though they live in continuous defiance of the Sixth Word.

Jesus doesn't forbid anger. Righteous outrage is real, as Jesus' action in the temple demonstrates. Jesus requires a righteousness that surpasses that of the scribes and Pharisees, a righteousness like Jesus' own (Matt 5:17–20). Jesus doesn't merely avoid wrong. His is an active righteousness that triumphs over evil.

What Jesus *commands* is a set of practices to defuse anger and overcome evil with good (Matt 5:21–26). If you're at odds with a brother, leave your offering at the altar and seek reconciliation. Stop the lawsuit; make friends quickly, out of court. Don't seek vengeance; turn the other cheek. The Sixth Word demands we be peacemakers, sons of God like *the* Son.

Second, the Sixth Word describes Jesus' *character and actions*. Jesus' entire life incarnates "Thou shalt not kill." He doesn't assault God's image, but restores it. He doesn't wound, but heals. He doesn't take life, but gives it, abundantly. He doesn't oppress, but liberates. His words, even his harshest ones, are words of life. He uses the sword of his tongue to defend the weak and to call the wicked to a repentance that leads to life.

Jesus has cause to defend himself and to seek vengeance. He has legions of angels at his command. Instead, Jesus gives himself, suffers in silent patience, loves and asks forgiveness for his executioners. He doesn't kill but dies a victim of murder, and so gives life. In the Sixth Word, he calls us to follow, to renounce every form of murder, to be martyrs who give ourselves and so become agents of his abundant life.

COMMANDMENT VII

THOU SHALT NOT COMMIT ADULTERY.

"THOU SHALT NOT COMMIT ADULTERY"

U nlike the permissive gods of antiquity and modernity, the God of Sinai is an intrusive God who won't leave us alone. He tells Israel that they must worship and serve him *alone*. He tells them *how* to worship him, without images. Ever the divine Micromanager, he schedules their week. Ever the divine Idealist, he expects us to live in the real world without violence and vengeance. In the tenth commandment, he really steps over the line and intrudes on thoughts and desires.

No commandment prickles more than the seventh. Many live by a creed of sexual autonomy: my body is my own, and my sexual desires, whatever they are, are normal and healthy. How dare the Lord—how dare *anyone*—interfere with my constitutional right to think and do and feel whatever I damn well please? Can I have a *little* privacy, please?

Of course, most are sane enough to acknowledge limits on sexual behavior. Few endorse sex with children, and only extreme progressives say the family should be given a quiet burial, along with the absurd notion of lifelong marital faithfulness. Most know that adultery is a bad deal and agree that society has to guard the family from the acid of infidelity. Adultery breaks up marriages and homes. Men and women suffer trauma and are impoverished by and after divorce. Children watch in horror as their parents battle at home, in court, over *them*, for years. We can't enjoy the goods of marriage if every man is on the prowl for his friend's wife and every wife is looking for a chance to slip away to a motel.

God isn't satisfied protecting the family. He prohibits other forms of sexual activity. Yahweh tells Israel who they can and cannot have sex with—not with one's mother or stepmother, daughter-in-law, sister, or aunt (Lev 18). Yahweh forbids men to lie with men as with women (Lev 18:22), and forbids sexual contact with animals (Lev 18:23). If a man has sex with a virgin, he'll soon have to face her father, who might demand marriage or a dowry (Exod 22:16–17). Yahweh doesn't consider consent the fundamental standard of sexual etiquette but prohibits forms of consensual sex between adults. How *dare* he?

Gentle Jesus makes things worse: "You have heard it said, Do not commit adultery. But I say to you, everyone who looks at a woman to lust after her has already committed adultery with her in his heart" (Matt 5:27–30). Jesus prohibits sexual desires and the habit of "checking out" that fuels desire. If you thought Jesus might leave a loophole, the option of watching porn in the privacy of your bedroom, you're wrong. You watch pornography to do *exactly* what Jesus forbids, to look at a woman or man to arouse lust.[94]

When all is said and done, the Bible demands that men and women channel our mercurial sexuality into a single narrow path: lifelong commitment in heterosexual marriage.

Recently, we've taken sexual autonomy several steps further by making our identity as male or female a matter of choice. Gender dysphoria is a painful burden, but difficult cases don't change the fundamental reality. Each of us has received the gift of being one or another sort of human being, male or female (Gen 1:26–28), a fact inscribed on our bodies. God calls us to be the kind of human being he made us to be. Men are called to the glorious vocation of being men, women to the high calling of being women. Both are called to submit to the order that God established for male and female.

Contrary to our cultural assumptions, there *is* an order to male and female: "The man was not made for the woman," Paul says, referring to Genesis 2, "but the woman for the sake of the man" (1 Cor 11:9). "Adam was first created, then Eve" (1 Tim 2:13). Paul highlights the mutuality of the sexes: Eve originated from Adam, but every man since has originated from a woman. All, male and female, come from God (1 Cor 11:11–12).

But mutual dependence doesn't make the sexes interchangeable. Mutuality exists alongside an order of first and second.

Yahweh treats sexual activity as a matter of *public* concern. In ancient Israel, some sexual sins were *crimes*. Adulterers—both the man and woman—are put to death (Lev 20:10). When a man lies with a man as with a woman, both are put to death (Lev 20:13). A man or woman who has sex with an animal is executed, and so is the animal (Lev 20:15–16). A man who sleeps with his mother, stepmother, or daughter-in-law is put to death (Lev 20:11–12).

However these laws apply to other nations, Paul makes it clear that the church publicly enforces sexual norms. The Corinthian man who has sex with his father's wife has to be handed to Satan in a church assembly (1 Cor 5:4). Paul quotes the death-penalty formula from Deuteronomy: "Remove the wicked man from among you" (1 Cor 5:13). The church doesn't use the civil sword. It enforces sexual norms with the far more powerful sword of church discipline.

Societies continue only if they reproduce, and reproduction takes place through sexual union of man and woman. Social order is bound up with bodily differences and sexual intercourse: "What I do in bed is the area of my action in which the community has the most urgent interest." A refusal to legislate here is insane, and dangerous. "No society," Robert Jenson writes, "can endure mere shapelessness." If our sexuality isn't shaped by customary or religious norms, the state will be happy to impose order.[95]

These social and political concerns don't get to the depth of the Seventh Word. Adultery isn't simply a lack of self-control, or unfaithfulness to an oath. The Seventh Word parallels the Second. As veneration of images is spiritual adultery, so adultery is a kind of idolatry. Adultery isn't merely a familial and social catastrophe. It's an assault on God's image.

Sex and marriage are theological realities from top to bottom. Paul wasn't imposing a Christ-and-church paradigm on the neutral natural phenomenon of sexual difference (Eph 5). Sex is created as a sign of God's love for his Bride. That's what it's *for*. That's why Paul quotes from Genesis 2: The great mystery is that God created man male and female, a differentiated unity and a unified differentiation, as a living sign of his covenant bond with his people.

The account of Eve's creation is an allegory of the covenant God and his people (Gen 2).[96] "It is not good for man to be alone," Yahweh says of Adam. That is: God has chosen not to be alone, but to be God for and with us. "A man shall leave his father and mother and cleave to his wife," Genesis says. Just so, the God of Israel leaves heaven to enter the valley of death to rescue his Bride. Marriage portrays incarnation. "The two shall become one flesh," Genesis says, in a union of life that expresses the one-Spirit union of Christ and the church. A man and a woman aren't married on weekdays and free on weekends, single during the day and married at night. Everything is colored by their marriage, which is as all-encompassing as God's covenant with Israel. "They were naked and not ashamed,"

Genesis tells us, and so offers hope of future intimacy when, in the new creation, our shame will be removed and we will be forever face-to-face, unveiled, with our Lord.

Every perverse form of sexuality distorts the created design of marriage. Adultery, Clement of Alexandria says, is like the betrayal of idolatry.[97] We seek sexual pleasure without a commitment to a shared life, and so defy the faithful covenant God. We try out multiple sexual partners, and thus live a lie about the God who loves *one* Bride. Homosexual acts shatter the union-in-difference at the heart of God's relation to his people. Sexual sin lies about the Creator. The created order is to be a manifestation of the Lord of the covenant.[98]

This is the logic of the prophetic imagery of sexual unfaithfulness.[99] At times, the prophets condemn the sexual behavior of individuals in Judah. More often, unfaithful Judah is the adulterous wife. Jesus uses the same imagery when he condemns the "evil and adulterous generation" (Matt 12:39; 16:4) that rejects him. James warns his readers not to be "adulteresses," friends of the world who are faithless to the divine Husband (Jas 4:4).

Once we see marriage and adultery in this theological perspective, the "Do nots" fall into place. All are rooted in the fundamental "Do": Be what you are as male and female. As a *married* husband and wife, be the living image of the God of creation and covenant.[100]

Sexual faithfulness in marriage and sexual purity outside of marriage aren't mere demands of law. Sexual faithfulness preaches the gospel. When a husband and wife are faithful to one another, sexually and otherwise, they become a created symbol of the covenant God who keeps his vows to Israel and the new Israel. By keeping the Seventh Word, we dramatize the good news of Jesus, the Bridegroom of the church, who gives himself in utter fidelity to and for his Bride.

THOU SHALT NOT STEAL.

"THOU SHALT NOT STEAL"

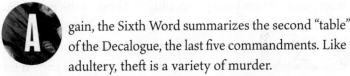

Again, the Sixth Word summarizes the second "table" of the Decalogue, the last five commandments. Like adultery, theft is a variety of murder.

This isn't obvious to us. We own our house, car, furniture, kitchenware, land, the odd family heirloom. But we don't think of them as part of our personality. They're tools, or toys.

There's biblical ground for that distinction. The Torah punishes crimes against persons differently from crimes against property. Murder is punished with a death penalty (Num 35), as is cursing father or mother (Exod 21:17; Lev 20:9). Some sexual acts are capital crimes (Lev 20). But the typical penalty for property crimes is restitution (Exod 22:1–5). You stole $100, so you have to give back $100 plus have $100 taken from you. It's eye for eye: you suffer the loss you imposed on your neighbor.[101]

Perhaps the connection of person and property was stronger when more people sewed their own clothes and built their own homes, or knew the craftsman who made their candlesticks and mixing bowls. In our economy, property is depersonalized. We don't make our own stuff. We dispose of things and buy new things readily, gleefully, greedily. Ring out the old, ring in the new.

Even so, we become emotionally attached to our things. What we *are* includes what we *have*. To own something is to incorporate it into your personality.[102] Think of the pride you take in a new car, home, sofa. Buy a beach house, and you become the sort of person who owns a beach house. Think of your affection for a car or piece of furniture you've owned for a long time. ("We've been through a *lot* together," you whisper when no one is looking.) Think of how you feel when something is stolen. You reassure yourself by saying, "Well, it's *just* a watch." But you can't shake the feeling that you've been violated—not just your stuff, but *you*.

The Bible hints at this connection between persons and property in various ways. In the Torah, the first specific law about theft is a prohibition of kidnapping or "man-stealing" (Exod 21:16). We can steal another person by enslaving him, unjustly imprisoning him, coercing his productivity, manipulating an employee to accept lower-than-reasonable pay.[103] Further, the law demands that we take care of our neighbor's property. If a friend gives you something to keep while he's on vacation, you must protect it as if it's your own (Exod 22:7). If you damage something you borrowed, you must make restitution (Exod 22:14). If you find your neighbor's animal wandering, you must return it or take care of it until the owner reclaims it (Deut 22). If your *enemy's* animal is caught under a burden, you must release and return it (Exod 23:4–5). You can't say, "I love my enemy, but I'm going to trash his stuff." The Golden Rule encompasses property as well as personal relations: you love your enemy by caring for his property as you would have him care for yours. Protecting your neighbor's things is *part of* love for him.

The connection of person and property is clearest with regard to God's property. Yahweh claims certain things as uniquely his. They are "holy things" or "most holy things" because they belong to God. God himself is holy, and his things participate in his holiness. God incorporates his things into his person. As images of God, the things we own become extensions of our persons.[104] We too have our "holy things" and "holy places."

Once we see the deep bonds we form with our possessions, we feel the full force of Jesus' teaching on wealth. He has no place to lay his head, and he calls disciples from their livelihoods to follow him. He tells the rich young ruler to give away everything. If possessions were loosely fitted add-ons, that would be easy. But it's not easy. Giving away our stuff is like cutting off a limb. Jesus' demand that we be ready to give up our possessions is the same as his demand that we be ready to give up our lives. In both cases, he calls us to *self*-renunciation.

You don't need to put panty hose over your face and sneak into a house to be a thief. You can steal in broad daylight, in the marketplace, whenever you defraud or deceive. Scripture demands honesty in weights and measures (Lev 19:35; Deut 25:15). Over time, ancient metal coins wear thin. A dishonest merchant could shave off layers of a silver coin; he claims the coin contains fifty shekels of silver, when it's only forty-five. That's theft, and it points to the importance of trust and trustworthiness in economic transactions. Much of our economic activity is mediated through language: promises, contracts, advertisements.[105] You can't say, "I'll be honest in conversation, but my contracts will be blurry around the edges."[106] As Thomas Aquinas said, we break the Eighth Word every time we defraud our neighbor in buying or selling.[107]

The eighth commandment parallels the third. Theft is practical idolatry, service to Mammon, one of our world's most revered idols. More than power, money is the god of Wall Street and K Street and Pennsylvania Avenue. Our polity is organized to maximize GDP. When disaster strikes, we do our patriotic duty by buying more stuff, enabled by smartphones that allow us to shop anytime, anywhere. Advertisements bombard us with enticements to believe, contrary to Jesus, that life consists in the abundance of possessions (Luke 12:15).

Worse, Christians have become utterly comfortable in Mammon's temples, pursuing dreams of unlimited prosperity:

"Who's hurt if money molds my life? I'm helping the economy grow, my kids get into the best schools, and I can buy the best dance and piano teachers." We don't recognize that Mammon is as deadly as any idol. Sooner or later, like every idol, it leaves us with speechless mouths, blind eyes, deaf ears.

Christians of earlier ages saw Mammon for what it is. Martin Luther excoriated market fraud with a serrated vehemence that might give Karl Marx pause. He attacked those "who turn the free public market into nothing but a carrion-pit and a robber's den. The poor are defrauded every day, and new burdens and higher prices are imposed. They all misused the market in their own arbitrary, defiant, arrogant way, as if it were their privilege and right to sell their goods as high as they please."[108]

Shatter Mammon. But *how*? Give all your goods to the poor? Join a commune or a monastery? Ultimately, we break Mammon's hold when we acknowledge that all we have is a gift from God. Our property is ours, but in the mode of gift. That's why property "rights" aren't absolute in Scripture. In ancient Israel, land returned to its original owners every fifty years (Lev 25). Farmers weren't allowed to maximize profit from their fields but left the corners of their fields to the landless poor (Lev 19:9; 23:22).[109] Dropped sheaves were left for gleaners, and grapes were reserved for the poor (Lev 19:9–10). Gathering dropped sheaves was stealing from the mouth of the hungry.

The principle holds for Christians: our material goods are like the gifts we receive from the Spirit. They're ours, but we possess them to edify the body. We don't give away everything, but we *do* use everything to bless. We're given material goods to advance God's justice.[110]

Once we reckon with God's universal ownership, we can see the story of fall and redemption shrouded within the Eighth Word. God created Adam to have dominion, to take ownership of creation. The fruit of the tree of knowledge was the one thing that belonged exclusively to God. Adam stole it, and all children of Adam are thieves, stealing God's holy things, assaulting God's image by assaulting the property of others.[111] Above all, we steal *ourselves* from God: We are not our own; we were bought at a price (1 Cor 6:19–20). We bear the Name that marks us as the Lord's property (Third Word), yet we want to be our own god. Every time we disobey, we steal and commit sacrilege, misusing God's holy things.

God didn't imprison Adam's son forever. He sent the Son, who, though existing in the form of God, did not think equality with God a thing to be grasped, seized, or stolen. Instead, he humbled, offered, and emptied himself. Though rich, he became poor that we might share in God's riches. He didn't steal, but gave. He repaid the debt *we* had incurred.

By the new-creative Word, the Spirit of this last, all-generous Adam makes us a new humanity. "Thou shalt not steal" is a character description of Jesus, and obedience to this command is obedience to the gospel, the call to imitate Jesus' labor and self-gift.

THOU SHALT NOT BEAR FALSE WITNESS AGAINST THY NEIGHBOR.

"THOU SHALT NOT BEAR FALSE WITNESS"

Christians sometimes read the Ten Words as "moral law," understood as the realm of individual ethics. These commandments do govern the lives of individuals. But Yahweh addresses his son, Israel, so that Israel's *corporate* life will conform to the word from Sinai. The ten new-creative words bring Israel's *social* life under the reign of God. Worship, timekeeping, parental and other authorities, the use of force, sexuality and family life, and property are all integrated into the covenant.[112] With the Ninth Word, courts of justice come into view.

The ninth commandment isn't, "Thou shalt not lie." It's more specific. It requires "witnesses" summoned to testify in court to tell the truth, the whole truth, and nothing but the truth. They must not be "witnesses of violence" (Exod 23:1; Deut 19:15–21). A false witness is a club, sword, and sharp arrow (Prov 25:18) who deploys the bludgeon of state power to murder his neighbor or damage his good name. We speak truth of and to our neighbors because they're made in God's image. To bear false witness is blasphemy against another human, as bearing God's name lightly is blasphemy against him.[113]

Elsewhere, the Torah deals with bribery, intimidation, and other forms of corruption (Exod 23:8; Deut 10:17; 16:19; 27:25). Court decisions shape social life, forcing changes in settled customs[114] and distributing rewards and demerits. If courts are controlled by money or violence, society will be molded by the wealthy, powerful, and malicious. To be just, society must be shaped by truth, centrally by truthful testimony and just decisions in courtroom settings.[115]

The Hebrew verb in the Ninth Word is normally translated as "answer."[116] In context, it connotes "answer a summons" or "answer a question posed in court." But it points to the larger truth that human speech is answering speech. Yahweh spoke to Adam before Adam spoke to Eve. Each of us was born speechless. We learn to speak only as we are spoken to.

That broadens out the Ninth Word. It demands truthtelling in every setting, not merely under the formal procedures of a court of law. As Martin Luther said, it prohibits betrayal, slander, the spreading of evil rumors.[117] True words can destroy, when spoken as gossip. Few themes are more prominent in

Proverbs than the wise use of the tongue. Too much speech is dangerous (Prov 10:8). Timing is all the difference between rotten words and verbal apples of gold in settings of silver (Prov 25:11). Sweet speech is dangerously seductive (Prov 5:3), but for the same reason it can persuade kings (Prov 16:21; 22:11). Smooth speech enables the ambitious to steal hearts (see Absalom, 2 Sam 15:6). Deception is a lubricant of social life, from excusable courtesies to self-serving flattery, which has been called the most harmful of lies.[118] We rarely sin without a backup plan in case we get caught: "I can always lie my way out of this."

The Ninth Word is a fitting word for our mediated age. We're spun by a whirlpool of rumor, innuendo, false accusation, slander, libel. People are tried and condemned by online lynch mobs. We like or share Tweets and Facebook posts even though we can't possibly confirm their accuracy. Luther said that the Ninth Word requires us to put "the best construction on everything," to give others the benefit of the doubt. We exaggerate the stupidity or malevolence of ideological adversaries to score points and win honor in Twitter combat. Officially committed to the Ten Words, the church does no better. Christians fire up the digital kindling to burn supposed heretics without due process, humility, or care.

This isn't merely an improper *use* of neutral technology. YouTube gives preference to controversial videos, the more outlandish the better. Twitter is a medium of self-presentation, often self-preening, where every user plays a game of "brand management."[119] Not by accident but by design, social media encourages violations of the Ninth Word.

Lies can become embedded in the foundations of a culture. When a member of the Toraja tribe sets out in his canoe, he tricks the gods by saying, in a loud voice, that he's planning a canoe trip *tomorrow*. No Toraja will compliment a pretty girl, for fear that jealous gods will give her the face of a dog.[120] We smile at the primitive superstition, but in living memory much of Eastern Europe lived under a regime of lies. As Vaclav Havel memorably put it, "Because the regime is captive to its own lies, it must falsify everything. It falsifies the past. It falsifies the present, and it falsifies the future. It falsifies statistics. It pretends not to possess an omnipotent and unprincipled police apparatus. It pretends to respect human rights. It pretends to persecute no one. It pretends to fear nothing. It pretends to pretend nothing." The Soviet bloc crumbled when truth-tellers like Havel and John Paul II uttered the simple, childlike words, "The empire has no clothes."[121]

The Ninth Word parallels the Fourth, the Sabbath command. On the Lord's Day, we confess the Truth that is Jesus Christ, hear the truth from Scripture and sermon, sing the truth. The liturgy trains us in truth-telling. It forms the church as a truth-living people, sons of the Father through the eternal Son.

Truth-telling isn't necessarily "nice." We learn to be truth-tellers when we learn to see clearly and when we break the habit of covering our cowardice with the pious excuse of "love."[122] Immediately after Yahweh forbids Israelites to hate their countrymen (Lev 19:17) and immediately before he tells them to "love your neighbor as yourself" (Lev 19:18), he tells them to "reprove your neighbor" (Lev 19:17 NASB). Prophets like Nathan (2 Sam 12) and Elijah (1 Kgs 17–19) weren't nice. They really performed the cliché: they spoke truth to power. And their blistering words carried divine power, to pluck up and plant, to demolish and build (cf. Jer 1:10). Truthful correction is an expression of love, not hate. If you tell the truth, you will create conflict, and then you are called to be a peacemaker. But true peace can be won only if the truth shatters the false peace of the lie.

Here we stumble on the flip side of today's social disorder. While we gleefully spread gossip on social media, we tiptoe gingerly around the truth. We say we're tolerant and want to avoid triggering. But we're cowards, and hateful cowards to boot. If we can't tell the truth, we cannot identify real evils. If we're forbidden to name problems, we cannot propose solutions.

The second half of the Decalogue deals with love for the "neighbor," but the elusive neighbor comes out of hiding for the first time in the Ninth Word. That tells us something about neighborly relations. We may have a fairly easy time avoiding murder, adultery, theft. Most of us don't get into fistfights with our neighbors or slip a silver fork into our pocket during a dinner party. Most of our interactions with neighbors take place in speech. Wisely, the Lord's first explicit test of our love of our neighbors is, How do we speak about and to them?

The Ninth Word forbids us to answer falsely against our neighbor or "friend." What about enemies? Are we free to answer with false testimony? Augustine was an absolutist: lying is never justified.[123] But Scripture's heroes often deceive their enemies. The Hebrew midwives lie to protect infant boys (Exod 1); Rahab betrays soldiers of her own king to protect Israelite spies (Josh 2; see Jas 2); Jael pretends to offer Sisera a safe tent while intending to split his skull with a tent peg (Judg 4). After a string of female deceivers, we have David, who repeatedly misleads to escape from Saul, Achish, and others. These righteous deceptions all take place in wartime, and typically protect innocent life. They reflect God's justice: At the beginning, the serpent deceived Eve so that she ate from the tree. From that time on, new Eves have turned it back on the serpent's head, eye for eye, lie for lie.

But these are exceptions. Truthful speech is an act of love, and we are to love enemies as well as friends. In all normal circumstances, we speak truth to and about our enemies, refusing to minimize their virtues or exaggerate their faults.

Like the others, the Ninth Word is about Jesus, the true and faithful Witness. He speaks the truth during his life, arousing his enemies' murderous rage. He speaks the truth to skeptical Pilate. As Witness, he summons us as witnesses who answer truthfully about the hope within us, the living Hope that is Jesus himself. He calls us to speak truth no matter what the cost, to love truth more than life. With the Ninth Word, Jesus calls us to martyrdom.[124]

Martyrs aren't losers. Martyrdom is indefeasible. Martyrs speak world-shattering truth on the way to their world-shattering, world-renewing deaths. The Ninth Word is the Creator's command. He is Lord of our tongues. It is also a promise, the Lord's pledge to truthful witnesses: at the last judgment if not before, the truth will out and truthful witnesses will be vindicated.

COMMANDMENT X

THOU SHALT NOT COVET.

"THOU SHALT NOT COVET"

Stylistically, the Tenth Word is a surprise. In Hebrew, commandments 6–8 consist of two words each, "not" plus a verb. The ninth commandment is loquacious by comparison, with five words. Then the Tenth Word, which has more words (fifteen) than the rest of the second table combined (eleven). It didn't need to be so long. It says "do not covet" twice, and it lists the neighbor's goods in three pairs—house/wife, manservant/maidservant, ox/donkey—and then completes the list with a seventh item, "anything." Why not cut to the chase and say, "Thou shalt not covet anything of your neighbor's"? The doubled verb and the list remind us of the Sabbath command. The stylistic parallel suggests a substantive one: we give Sabbath rest by mortifying our covetous desires.

The Tenth Word is one of two that appears in a significantly different form in Deuteronomy 5. In Exodus 20, the Sabbath command is rooted in creation, while in Deuteronomy Israel keeps Sabbath because Yahweh rescued them from Egypt. The change in the tenth commandment is more subtle. Exodus prohibits coveting the neighbor's house, and then his wife. Deuteronomy reverses the order: "Thou shalt not covet thy neighbor's wife; thou shalt not covet thy neighbor's house" (Deut 5:21). Exodus treats the wife as part of the household; Deuteronomy elevates the wife above the house.

This shift is consistent with the movement of the Torah and biblical history as a whole, an elevation of the bride. The first census in Numbers (Num 1) counts male warriors, but the second, taken after the first Israel has died in the wilderness, numbers according to "families" and includes women and children (Num 26). Numbers ends by reiterating Moses' ruling concerning the inheritance of the daughters of Zelophehad (Num 36). Other covenants have a first "husbandly" phase, then a bridal second phase: first Elijah alone, then Elisha with his company of prophets; first Jesus, then the apostles and the church. Biblical history, and each phase of biblical history, moves from Adam to Adam-and-Eve, from the Last Adam to the Last Adam with his Bride.

The Tenth Word regulates "desire." Covetousness isn't the same as jealousy or envy. Jealousy is a proper protectiveness for what is ours. Distorted, it becomes miserly. Envy is corrosive hatred for another's success or wealth, which seeks an outlet in verbal or physical violence. An envious man may not physically deface his neighbor's stylish home or subvert his business; he'll take every opportunity to defame his neighbor and degrade his house. The jealous hoard, the envious kill, the covetous steal.

Like bodies, societies thrive when different parts contribute to the whole. Eyes serve the body by seeing, hands by grasping, legs and feet by walking. In a healthy society, wisdom, authority, and experience will be honored. The Fifth Word demands that we honor and preserve these hierarchies. Covetousness, envy, and jealousy erode social differentiations. The covetous hand desires the eye's power of sight; the envious ear wants the whole body to be an ear.

Desire is fundamental to biblical anthropology, its understanding of human existence. We think, but we aren't primarily thinking things. We're *desiring* beings. Like the animals, Adam was made a "living soul" (Gen 2:7; cf. 1:20–21, 24, 30). Our souls move us to action, and souls move us by desire (1 Sam 23:20; Job 23:13; Eccl 6:2, 9). Sexual desire is a longing of soul (Gen 34:8), hunger and thirst arise from the soul (Ps 107:9), and the yearning for God's presence is a desire of the soul (Ps 42:1–2; 63:1; 84:2; 143:6; Isa 26:9). Dante was right: everything we do is motivated by proper or distorted love.[125] Desire is the combustible power that moves human life.

Desires are inseparable from evaluations of the desirability of the thing desired. God made trees "desirable to the eyes" (Gen 2:9), and eyes are organs of judgment and evaluation. Eve "saw" the tree was desirable to make one wise, and so she ate

(Gen 3:6). Desire moves us to take the object of desire—food, a sexually attractive person, our neighbor's shiny Porsche—and to incorporate it into ourselves.

The Bible acknowledges the disruptive, dangerous power of desire, and Christians developed the notion of seven deadly sins to warn against disfigured desire. But desire isn't evil because it's strong. Desire becomes evil when it's fixed on the wrong objects, when we misevaluate the desirability of something. Eve covets the fruit and takes it, Shechem desires Dinah and seduces her (Gen 34), and Achan covets the treasure of Jericho and steals it from Yahweh (Josh 7:21). Evil desire lays traps (e.g., Deut 7:25). This is why Paul says covetousness is idolatry (Col 3). Our souls impel us to seek satisfactions in things that we *wrongly* judge to be satisfying.

We avoid the trap not by suppressing desire, but by learning to see past the fizzy surface of things. We avoid Lady Folly's trap when we see that her beauty—which is *real* beauty—is a death mask (Prov 6:25). The Bible doesn't teach us to master, control, or kill desire. Our desires are to *mature*, so that our souls, brought to life by the Spirit, move us to pursue *real* treasure and eternal glory *with passion*.

We mimic the desires of others, and sometimes catch their desires as if they were a contagious infection.[126] Desires take cultural, institutional, political forms that shape our souls. Consumer culture is organized to entice desire for all the wrong things. Advertisers try to convince us that this or that food, drink, show, car, vacation is desirable to make one happy. As

Ferdinand Mount has pointed out, the seven deadly sins have been given a positive spin: "Covetousness has been rebranded as retail therapy, sloth as downtime, lust is exploring your sexuality, anger is opening up your feelings, vanity is looking good because you're worth it and gluttony is the religion of foodies."[127] What Christians once saw as deadly desires are now the very things that make the world go round.

More subtly, our culture encourages us to think our desires are free. We desire what we desire because we choose to. Or, in an even narrower circle, we desire what we desire because we desire it. Such absolutist notions of freedom are self-contradictory. By our cultural logic, if freedom is limited by anything beyond our known will and desire, then freedom is no longer absolute. But desire is *itself* a limit. When I hunger or thirst, I seek *particular* satisfactions—food and drink. Sexual desire impels toward sexual gratification. Desires can be diverted, repressed, masked, but they retain the same structure. Desire is ordered to ends, tethered to a telos. "Freedom to do whatever I desire" mangles this structure. It leaves desire end-less.

Desire is free only when it's directed toward an object. The Russian poet Vera Pavlova expresses this in an arresting poem:

I am in love, hence free to live
by heart, to improvise caresses.
A soul is light when full,
heavy when vacuous.
My soul is light. She is not afraid

> to dance the agony alone,
> for I was born wearing your shirt,
> will come from the dead with that shirt on.[128]

Pavlova links being to freedom: "I am … hence free." But a specific experience links them: love. Contrary to cynics of all ages, Pavlova insists that love need not be bondage, but can liberate. Liberated by love, she is free to live "by heart" and to "improvise caresses." Her spontaneity isn't spontaneous. It bubbles up as a by-product of love's bond.

As the poem continues, "heart" modulates into "soul," and the poet introduces a paradox of soul and body. Full bodies are heavy, empty bodies light. Souls, by contrast, are not weighed down by being full; rather, the fuller they are, the lighter, airier, and more ethereal they become. Love lightens the soul, freeing it to live by heart, while a loveless soul is as heavy and earthbound as an overstuffed stomach. Even the prospect of death doesn't weigh down the lover's soul. Love will bring her from death wearing her lover's shirt.

Desire is liberating not *in spite of* its fixity but *because of* its fixity. "Follow your heart" is paralyzing advice to someone whose eyes are dazzled by every passing beauty, whose vacuous soul is blown about by the most recent Tweet. Living by heart is freeing *only* for someone whose heart is already taken. Lovers alone are free to act spontaneously without risk that spontaneity will collapse into the absolute freedom that is indistinguishable from nihilism.

We're in Augustinian territory, where the key is to order desires *rightly*, to direct our loves at lovable things that deserve our fixed love. From this Augustinian perspective, we are genuinely free only if our desires are trained, only if we have been brought out of the Egypt of self-love to embrace proper objects of love.

Yahweh liberated his son Israel, and he wants his son to live in freedom—free from tyrannical gods, free from idols, free to rejoice, free from fear of violence, seduction, theft, rumor, and gossip. These freedoms are achieved, however, only if the *souls* of Israel are free, free from evil desires and fixed on true riches.

This the law cannot give. It cannot grant the freedom it commands and commends. Augustine, alluding to Paul (Rom 7), notes that the law provokes a desire to break it. We don't even know that our desires are evil until the law brings them to light: "You started to make an effort to overcome what was inside, and what was hidden came to light."[129]

To be true sons, we need another Pentecost beyond Sinai, when the Spirit writes on human hearts. Then we'll fulfill Jesus' teaching: "Where your treasure is, there will your heart be also" (Matt 6:21 KJV). That describes Jesus' life of filial freedom, his soul hungering and thirsting for his Father's pleasure. In the Tenth Word, he calls us to the same freedom. Life is a treasure hunt. We seek a place to place our hearts, where we find the weighty treasures that lighten our souls.

ENDNOTES

1. See Christopher R. Seitz, "The Ten Commandments: Positive and Natural Law and the Covenants Old and New—Christian Use of the Decalogue and Moral Law," in *I Am the Lord Your God: Christian Reflections on the Ten Commandments*, ed. Carl E. Braaten and Christopher R. Seitz (Grand Rapids: Eerdmans, 2005), 18–38.

2. "Yahweh" transliterates God's name, which is also represented by YHWH. It's often rendered as LORD or Lord. Since it's a personal name, not a title, I have chosen to transliterate it.

3. Clement of Alexandria (*Stromata* 6.16) links ten to creation, listing "Decalogues" of heaven, earth, and human nature.

4. Origen links Sinai's third day to Jesus' resurrection in *Homilies on Genesis* 8.4.

5. Victor P. Hamilton, *Exodus: An Exegetical Commentary* (Grand Rapids: Baker Academic, 2011), 64.

6. In sixteenth-century English, "thou" was singular and "you" or "ye" plural.

7. Yahweh's command to Adam was also delivered on a mountain, Eden (Ezek 28:13–14).

8. Edward L. Greenstein, "The Rhetoric of the Ten Commandments," in *The Decalogue in Jewish and Christian Traditions*, ed. Hennig Graf

Reventlow and Yair Hoffman (London: T&T Clark, 2011), 11. See Stanley M. Hauerwas and William H. Willimon, *The Truth about God: The Ten Commandments in Christian Life* (Nashville: Abingdon, 1999), 19.

9. Thomas Aquinas points out that denials are more open-ended than affirmations. If you say, "It's white," you deny it's black. If you say, "It's not black," it could be white, red, blue, yellow, or orange (*Summa Theologiae* I–II, q. 100, art. 7).

10. John Wesley applies the words of Hebrews to the law: Like Jesus, the law is "the express image of his glory." Wesley concludes that the law is "divine virtue and wisdom in a visible form." Quoted in D. Stephen Long, "John Wesley," in *The Decalogue through the Centuries: From the Hebrew Scriptures to Benedict XVI*, ed. Jeffrey P. Greenman and Timothy Larsen (Louisville: Westminster John Knox, 2012), 174. Clement of Alexandria offers an imaginative numero-alphabetic interpretation: *yod* is the tenth letter of the Hebrew alphabet and the first letter of "Jeshua." Hence: the Ten Words speak of Jesus the Word (*Stromata* 6.16).

11. Augustine, *Against Faustus* 22.24.

12. Irenaeus, *Against Heresies* 4.16.6.

13. Augustine, *Sermon* 155.6.

14. See my discussion in "Don't Do, Don't Desire," Theopolis Institute, January 7, 2019, https://theopolisinstitute.com/leithart/dont-do-dont-desire.

15. Cited in Thomas Aquinas, *Summa Theologiae* I–II, q. 100, art. 4. Thomas agrees with Augustine.

16. Origen, *Homily 8 on Exodus*.

17. For a defense of Augustine, see Jason S. DeRouchie, "Counting the Ten: An Investigation into the Numbering of the Decalogue," in *For Our Good Always: Studies on the Message and Influence of Deuteronomy in Honor of Daniel I. Block*, ed. Jason S. DeRouchie, Jason Gile, and Kenneth J. Turner (Winona Lake, IN: Eisenbrauns, 2013), 93–125. See my response: "Counting to Ten," Theopolis Institute, February 18, 2019, https://theopolisinstitute.com/leithart/counting-to-ten.

18. Caesarius of Arles, *Sermon* 100a.

19. Meredith G. Kline, "The Two Tables of the Covenant," *Westminster Theological Journal* 22 (1960): 133–46.

20. So Philo, *De Decalogo*, cited in Paul Grimley Kuntz, *The Ten Commandments in History: Mosaic Paradigms for a Well-Ordered Society* (Grand Rapids: Eerdmans, 2004), 16–17.

21. In Hebrew, each letter has a numerical value. A gematria is the numerical sum of the letters of a word. Twenty-six is the gematria of "YHWH."

22. The first five words form a chiastic unit of their own: Peter Leithart, "Chiasm of Five Words," Theopolis Institute, November 29, 2018, https://theopolisinstitute.com/leithart/chiasm-of-five-words.

23. See Eduard Nielsen, *The Ten Commandments in New Perspective* (Naperville, IL: Alex R. Allenson, 1968).

24. Two angels visit Sodom, Moses and Aaron witness before Pharaoh, Elijah and Elisha call Ahab to repentance, two witnesses appear in the city where the Lord was crucified (Rev 11).

25. Justin, *Dialogue with Trypho the Jew* 93.10.

26. Irenaeus, *Against Heresies* 4.16.3–4.

27. Augustine, *On Faith and Works* 11.17.

28. Bernd Wannenwetsch speaks of the "perichoretic" character of the Decalogue, each commandment indwelt by the others ("You Shall Not Kill," 148). See also John M. Frame, *The Doctrine of the Christian Life* (Phillipsburg, NJ: P&R, 2008), who sees each individual commandment as a "perspective" on the whole.

29. Martin Luther, Lecture on Genesis 39:15 (WA 44:369.5–6), quoted in Wannenwetsch, "You Shall Not Kill," 162n46.

30. The phrase is from G. K. Beale, *We Become What We Worship: A Biblical Theology of Idolatry* (Downers Grove, IL: IVP Academic, 2008), 41.

31. Thomas Aquinas, *Summa Theologiae* I–II, q. 100, art. 6.

32. Luther, *Large Catechism*, in *The Book of Concord*, ed. Robert Kolb and Timothy J. Wengert (Minneapolis: Fortress, 2000), cited in Timothy J. Wengert, "Martin Luther," 109. See also Luther, *Freedom of the Christian*: "Not by the doing of works but by believing do we glorify God and acknowledge that he is truthful. Therefore faith alone is the righteousness of a Christian and the fulfilling of all the commandments, for he who fulfils the First Commandment has no difficulty in fulfilling all the rest" (LW 31:353).

33. Moshe Halbertal and Avishai Margalit's *Idolatry*, trans. Naomi Gold-blum (Cambridge, MA: Harvard University Press, 1992), stresses the personal-relational element of idolatry.

34. Luther, *Small Catechism*, explanation of the first commandment.

35. The following paragraphs are indebted to David Powlison, "Idols of the Heart and 'Vanity Fair,'" *Journal of Biblical Counseling* 13, no. 2 (1995): 35–50.

36. David Bentley Hart, "God or Nothingness," in *I Am the Lord Your God: Christian Reflections on the Ten Commandments*, ed. Carl E. Braaten and Christopher R. Seitz (Grand Rapids: Eerdmans, 2005), 57–58.

37. Clement, *Stromata* 6.16.

38. Origen, *Exhortation to Martyrdom* 9.

39. Thus the Second and Seventh Words match each other, a hint that the first table of Five Words matches the second table. Moshe Halbertal and Avishai Margalit observe that adultery is the main biblical image for idolatry (*Idolatry*, trans. Naomi Goldblum [Cambridge, MA: Harvard University Press, 1992]). In the ancient world, images also had political uses. In prohibiting images, Yahweh forbids Israel to enter alliances with idolaters. See Gary North, *The Sinai Strategy: Economics and the Ten Commandments* (Tyler, TX: Institute for Christian Economics, 1986), 29–38.

40. Luther, *Large Catechism* in *Book of Concord*. According to the enumeration Luther follows, this blessing and curse is attached to the first commandment.

41. Luther even called the ear *the* Christian organ. Lecture on Hebrews 10:5 (LW 29:224).

42. Guy Debord, *Society of the Spectacle*, trans. Ken Knabb (London: Rebel Press, 2004).

43. Halbertal and Margalit, *Idolatry*, 37–66.

44. "God of Abraham, Isaac, and Jacob" is nearly Yahweh's surname.

45. Origen, *On Prayer* 24.2–3.

46. Eusebius (*Proof of the Gospel* 5.16.243) sees a hint of the Father-Son relation in the Ten Words. Yahweh first speaks of himself as "I Yahweh," then of his name in the third person. Eusebius writes, "The second Lord is here mystically instructing his servant about the Father."

47. See Patrick D. Miller, *The Ten Commandments*, Interpretation: Resources for the Use of Scripture in the Church (Louisville: Westminster John Knox, 2009), 65, 68.

48. Hauerwas and Willimon, *Truth about God*, 47.

49. Miller, *Ten Commandments*, 82, 87, 97.

50. The verb "bear" is used in Exod 19:4, where Yahweh says he "carried" Israel to Sinai on eagle's wings. Because he bore them, they are to bear him. Elsewhere in Exodus, the verb means "forgive" or "pardon" (Exod 32:32; 34:7). Yahweh has carried away Israel's sins, and for that reason they bear his name.

51. Ephraim Radner has explored this shift in "Taking the Lord's Name in Vain," 77–84.

52. I'm riffing on Ephraim Radner, "Taking the Lord's Name in Vain," 84–94.

53. Rabanus Maurus, *Commentary on Exodus*, cited in Radner, "Taking the Lord's Name in Vain," 92.

54. The phrase is from Ramon Lull, *De proverbiis moralibus, tertia pars caput VIII–Caput XVII, tome II*, in *Opera omnia* 42 (Mainz, 1721; repr., Frankfurt am Main: Minerva, 1965), quoted in Kuntz, *Ten Commandments in History*, 53.

55. Miller, *Ten Commandments*, 118.

56. Augustine, *Sermon* 8.6; *Letter* 55; *Tractate on John* 20.2.

57. Caesarius of Arles, *Sermon* 100.4.

58. Augustine, *Sermon* 179a.

59. Bede, *Homilies on the Gospels* 2.17.

60. See Karl Barth, *Church Dogmatics* III.4, §53.1 (p. 72): "He who has a self-renouncing faith on Sunday will have it also on a week-day. In the week he may and will work conscientiously and industriously, but neither as the lord nor as the slave of his work. ... In the week he will have to fix his eyes on one aim after another, yet not fall under the dominion of any material or spiritual, individual or collective Mammon. As he is busy on the everyday, he will also rest; as he fights on the everyday, he will also be at peace; as he works on the everyday, he will also pray."

61. "Interrupt" is from Barth, *Church Dogmatics* III.4, §53.1 (p. 50). Miller says that service of God is "routinized" by the Sabbath (*Ten Commandments*, 131).

62. Samson Raphael Hirsch, *Horeb: A Philosophy of Jewish Laws and Observances*, trans. I. Grunfeld, 2 vols. in 1 (New York: Soncino, 1962), 76–77.

63. David L. Baker, *Tight Fists or Open Hands? Wealth and Poverty in Old Testament Law* (Grand Rapids: Eerdmans, 2009), 294.

64. Miller, *Ten Commandments*, 138.

65. Joseph Ratzinger, *Collected Works*, vol. 2, *Theology of the Liturgy: The Sacramental Foundation of Christian Existence*, ed. Michael J. Miller, trans. John Saward et al. (San Francisco: Ignatius, 2014), 198–99.

66. Stanley Hauerwas and William Willimon, *The Truth about God: The Ten Commandments in Christian Life* (Nashville: Abingdon, 1999), 59.

67. Hauerwas and Willimon, *Truth about God*, 64.

68. Abraham J. Heschel, "A Palace in Time," in *The Ten Commandments: The Reciprocity of Faithfulness*, ed. William P. Brown (Louisville: Westminster John Knox, 2004), 214–22.

69. Thomas Aquinas, *Summa Theologiae* I–II, q. 100, art. 5.

70. Miller puts it nicely: The ethic of response is also an ethic of correspondence (*Ten Commandments*, 125).

71. Miller, *Ten Commandments*, 202.

72. According to the *Westminster Larger Catechism* (q. 124), "father and mother" represents "not only natural parents, but all superiors in age and gifts; and especially such as, by God's ordinance, are over us in place of authority, whether in family, church, or commonwealth." Luther agrees that the commandment refers to "parents and other authorities" (*Small Catechism*).

73. This implies also that civil, social, church, and economic leaders should rule with quasi-parental solicitude.

74. "Father *and* mother" is a biblical refrain (Exod 21:15; Prov 1:8; 6:20; 15:20; 30:17). If the father is king, the mother is queen.

75. Barth, *Church Dogmatics* III.4, §54.2 (p. 245).

76. Barth, *Church Dogmatics* III.4, §54.2 (pp. 255–59).

77. Patristic writers commonly assume that the commandment addresses adults. Honoring parents, Origen says, includes sharing "the necessaries of life, such as food and clothing" (*Commentary on Matthew* 11.9). See also Ambrose, *The Patriarchs* 1.1; Jerome, *Letter* 123.6; Augustine, *Sermon*

45.2. See Miller, *Ten Commandments*, 170–74; Hauerwas and Willimon, *Truth about God*, 71.

78. Note the order!

79. See Miller, *Ten Commandments*, 172–73.

80. Miller, *Ten Commandments*, 184.

81. Who is Israel's mother? Israel is "son," but also "bride" of Yahweh and "mother" of her children. Honoring the mother means honoring the traditions, habits, reputation of the people of God. Specifically, it means honoring leaders, who serve as "nursemaids" to the people (Num 11:12). Moses asks: Did I conceive and bring forth this people? (Num 11:12). The answer is no, and the implication is that Yahweh is "mother" as well as Father of Israel. Clement of Alexandria suggests that Wisdom is Israel's mother (*Stromata* 6.16).

82. Samson Raphael Hirsch writes that human beings are temples of the living God, and we dare not attack God's holy house (*Horeb*, 224). Philo too saw murder as sacrilegious theft "from its sanctuary of the most sacred of God's possessions," cited in Kuntz, *Ten Commandments in History*, 19.

83. James B. Jordan, *Studies in Exodus: Lecture Notes* (Niceville, FL: Biblical Horizons, 1992), 65.

84. See Miller, *Ten Commandments*, 224–31.

85. Augustine, *On Lying* 13.23. Thomas Aquinas agrees (*Summa Theologiae* I–II, q. 100, art. 8): The commandment prohibits undue killing, but the death penalty is *not* undue killing.

86. See Miller, *Ten Commandments*, 234–38.

87. Cavanaugh, "Killing in the Name of God," 127–47, esp. 131.

88. Hauerwas and Willimon, *Truth about God*, 80.

89. Hauerwas and Willimon, *Truth about God*, 87. See also the searing analysis in various books by Andrew Bacevich.

90. Cavanaugh, "Killing in the Name of God," 147.

91. Bernd Wannenwetsch, "You Shall Not Kill," 168–69.

92. Robert W. Jenson, *Systematic Theology*, vol. 2, *The Works of God* (Oxford: Oxford University Press, 1999), 88.

93. Cited in Wannenwetsch, "You Shall Not Kill," 152–53, 156.

94. As John Paul II put it, pornography detaches desire for the body from the "spousal" meaning of the body. Our bodies are designed for personal union, not for masturbatory pleasure.

95. Jenson, *Works of God*, 88–91.

96. The following paragraph depends on Karl Barth, *Church Dogmatics* III.4.

97. Clement, *Stromata* 6.16.

98. Jenson, "Male and Female He Created Them," 187.

99. Adultery is mentioned in the prophets far more than in the Torah (Isa 57:3; cf. Jer 3:8–9; Ezek 16, 23).

100. According to Thomas Aquinas, this is the deep rationale for the Bible's prohibition of premarital sex. An adulterous man doesn't give a body that belongs to his wife to his mistress. He gives "the body of Christ" that was given at baptism. If a man must not betray his wife, "with much more reason must he not be unfaithful to Christ?" (Thomas, *Catechetical Instructions* 102, cited in Hauerwas and Willimon, *Truth about God*, 94).

101. This is preferable to imprisonment. If I go to prison for stealing $100, the victim never gets his $100 back, and I pay far more than $100 in time, loss of reputation, despair, criminalization. I pay "debt to society," but I never pay what I owe to the victim. Restitution punishes the criminal in proportion to his crime *and* protects the rights of victims.

102. Hirsch, *Horeb*, 233.

103. Miller, *Ten Commandments*, 319.

104. We get a glimpse of this in the laws of purity. A person becomes unclean because of various bodily functions (Lev 15), or by contact with an animal carcass or a dead body (Lev 11; Num 19). A person's *clothing* also becomes unclean, so that when he cleanses himself, he has to wash his clothes as well as his body. Houses can also be defiled by mold or "leprosy" (Lev 14). Clothing and living spaces are extensions of persons, and share in the state of purity or impurity.

105. Did you read the fine print when you signed up for Facebook?

106. Hirsch, *Horeb*, 236, emphasizes the necessity of truthful words in economic life.

107. Thomas Aquinas, *Summa Theologiae* II-II, q. 66. Cited in Hauerwas and Willimon, *Truth about God*, 106.

108. Quoted in Wengert, "Martin Luther," 116.

109. Miller, *Ten Commandments*, 322, 329.

110. Hirsch, *Horeb*, 249.

111. Clement of Alexandria accused the astrologers of his day of theft because they stole control of fortune from God and gave it to the stars (*Stromata* 6.16).

112. Brueggemann, "Truth-Telling," 292.

113. Miller, *Ten Commandments*, 344–45.

114. Think of the dramatic effect of America's civil rights laws and court decisions, especially in the South.

115. Brueggemann, "Truth-Telling," 293.

116. A point made by Hirsch, *Horeb*, 265. See my exploration of the usage at "False Answer," Theopolis Institute, December 7, 2018, https://theopolisinstitute.com/leithart/false-answer.

117. Martin Luther, *Small Catechism*.

118. Hirsch, *Horeb*, 251.

119. The notion that social media use is "brand management" comes from my Theopolis colleague Alastair Roberts.

120. This is from the work of A. C. Kruyt, cited by J. Douma, *The Ten Commandments: Manual for the Christian Life*, trans. Nelson D. Kloosterman (Phillipsburg, NJ: P&R, 1996), 322–23.

121. Vaclav Havel, "The Power of the Powerless," history.hanover.edu/courses/excerpts/165havel.html.

122. Hauerwas and Willimon, *Truth about God*, 120.

123. Augustine, *On Lying*. See his statement, e.g., in 5.6. Paul J. Griffiths defends and updates Augustine's position in *Lying: An Augustinian Theology of Duplicity* (Eugene, OR: Wipf & Stock, 2010). In contrast, Jerome distinguished lying into three categories (malicious, useful, humorous), only one of which was wrong (malicious). See Augustine, *Letter* 28 to Jerome and Jerome's commentary on Gal 2:11–14.

124. Hauerwas and Willimon, *Truth about God*, 124.

THE TEN COMMANDMENTS

125. Dante, *Purgatorio*, canto 17.

126. The modern prophet of "mimetic desire" is René Girard.

127. Ferdinand Mount, *Full Circle: How the Classical World Came Back to Us* (New York: Simon & Schuster, 2010).

128. Vera Pavlova, "I am in love, hence free to live," trans. Steven Seymour, *Poetry*, January 2010, https://www.poetryfoundation.org/poetrymagazine/poems/53191/i-am-in-love-hence-free-to-live.

129. Augustine, *Sermon* 26.9.

TRANSLATIONS USED

Ambrose. *The Patriarchs*. In Ambrose, *Seven Exegetical Works*. Fathers of
the Church, vol. 65. Translated by Michael McHugh. Washington,
DC: Catholic University of American Press, 1970.

Augustine. *On Lying*. In Augustine, *Treatises on Various Subjects*. Fathers
of the Church, vol. 16. Translated by Mary Sarah Muldowney.
Washington, DC: Catholic University of America Press, 1952.

——. *Against Faustus*. Augustus, *Answer to Faustus, A Manichean*. Works of
St. Augustine: A Translation for the 21st Century. Translated by
Elizabeth Ruth Obbard. Hyde Park, NY: New City Press, 2007.

——. *Sermon 8*. In Augustine, *Sermons 1–19 on the Old Testament*. Works of
St. Augustine: A Translation for the 21st Century. Translated by
Edmund Hill. Hyde Park, NY: New City Press, 2003.

——. *Sermon 26*. In Augustine, *Sermons 20–50 on the Old Testament*. Works
of St. Augustine: A Translation for the 21st Century. Translated by
Edmund Hill. Hyde Park, NY: New City Press, 1991.

——. *Sermon 45*. In Augustine, *Sermons 20–50 on the Old Testament*. Works
of St. Augustine: A Translation for the 21st Century. Translated by
Edmund Hill. Hyde Park, NY: New City Press, 1991.

———. *Sermon 155*. In Augustine, *Sermons (148–183)*. Works of St. Augustine: A Translation for the 21st Century. Translated by Edmund Hill. Hyde Park, NY: New City Press, 1992.

———. *Letter 28*. In Augustine, *Letters 1–99*. Works of St. Augustine: A Translation for the 21st Century. Translated by Roland Teske. Hyde Park, NY: New City Press, 2001.

———. *Letter 55*. In Augustine, *Letters 1–99*. Works of St. Augustine: A Translation for the 21st Century. Translated by Roland Teske. Hyde Park, NY: New City Press, 2001.

———. *Tractate*. In Augustine, *Homilies on the Gospel of John, 1–40*. Works of St. Augustine: A Translation for the 21st Century. Translated by Edmund Hill. Hyde Park, NY: New City Press, 2009.

———. *On Faith and Works*. *St. Augustine on Faith and Works*. Ancient Christian Writers 48. Translated by Gregory Lombardo. Mahwah, NJ: Paulist Press, 1988.

Barth, Karl. *Church Dogmatics*. III/4, *The Doctrine of Creation*. Translated by A. T. MacKay et al. London: T&T Clark, 2004.

Bede. *Homilies on the Gospels*. Translated by L. T. Martin and D. Hurst. 2 vols. Kalamzoo, MI: Cistercian Publications, 1990.

Caesarius of Arles. *Sermon 100a*. Cesarius, *Sermons 81–186*. Fathers of the Church. Translated by Mary Magdalene Muller. Washington, DC: Catholic University of America Press, 1964.

Clement of Alexandria. *Stromata*. A. Roberts and J. Donaldson, eds. *Ante-Nicene Fathers, vol. 2*. 10 vols. Buffalo, NY: Christian Literature, 1885–1896. Reprint Grand Rapids: Eerdmans, 1951–1956.

Dante. *Purgatorio*. Translated by Mark Musa. New York: Penguin, 2003.

Eusebius. *Proof of the Gospel*. Translated by W. J. Ferrar. London: SPCK, 1920.

Irenaeus. *Against Heresies*. A. Roberts and J. Donaldson, eds. *Ante-Nicene Fathers*, vol. 1. 10 vols. Buffalo, NY: Christian Literature, 1885–1896. Reprint Grand Rapids: Eerdmans, 1951–1956.

Jerome. *Letter 123*. *Nicene and Post-Nicene Fathers*, Second Series, Vol. 6. Translated by W. H. Fremantle, G. Lewis and W. G. Martley. Buffalo, NY: Christian Literature Publishing Co., 1893.

——. *Commentary on Galatians*. The Fathers of the Church Patristic Series. Translated by Andrew Cain. Washington, D.C.: The Catholic University of America Press, 2010.

Justin. *Dialogue with Trypho the Jew*. A. Roberts and J. Donaldson, eds. *Ante-Nicene Fathers, vol. 1*. 10 vols. Buffalo, NY: Christian Literature, 1885–1896. Reprint Grand Rapids: Eerdmans, 1951–1956.

Luther, Martin. *Luther's Small Catechism*. St. Louis: Concordia, 1986.

——. *Large Catechism*. In *The Book of Concord*, edited by Robert Kolb and Timothy Wengert, 379–480. Minneapolis: Fortress, 2000.

——. *Luther's Works*. Vol. 29, *Lectures on Titus, Philemon, and Hebrews*. Edited by Jaroslav Pelikan. St. Louis: Concordia, 1968.

——. *Luther's Works*. Vol. 7, *Lectures on Genesis, Chapters 38–44*. Edited by Jaroslav Pelikan. St. Louis: Concordia, 1965.

Philo. *De Decalogo*. *Works of Philo*. Translated by C. D. Yonge. Peabody, MA: Hendrickson, 1993.

Origen. *Commentary on Matthew*. Allan Menzies, ed., *Ante-Nicene Fathers, Vol. 9*. Buffalo, NY: Christian Literature Publishing Co., 1896.

——. *Exhortation to Martyrdom*. Origen, *Prayer and Exhortation to Martyrdom*. Translated by John J. O'Meara. New York, NY: Newman Press, 1954.

——. *Homilies on Genesis*. Origen, *Homilies on Genesis and Exodus*. Fathers of the Church. Washington, DC: Catholic University of America Press, 1982.

——. *Homily 8 on Exodus*. Origen, *Homilies on Genesis and Exodus*. Fathers of the Church. Washington, DC: Catholic University of America Press, 1982.

——. *On Prayer*. Origen, *Prayer and Exhortation to Martyrdom*. Translated by John J. O'Meara. New York, NY: Newman Press, 1954.

Thomas Aquinas. *Summa theologiae*. Fathers of the English Dominican Province, 1920. Online edition by Kevin Knight, 2017.

Westminster Larger Catechism. *The Westminster Confession of Faith and Catechisms*. Lawrenceville, GA: Christian Education and Publications Committee of the Presbyterian Church in America, 2007.

WORKS CITED

Baker, David L. *Tight Fists, Open Hands: Wealth and Poverty in Old Testament Law*. Grand Rapids: Eerdmans, 2009.

Beale, G. K. *We Become What We Worship: A Biblical Theology of Idolatry*. Downers Grove, IL: IVP Academic, 2008.

Brueggemann, Walter. "Truth-Telling as Subversive Obedience." In *The Ten Commandments: The Reciprocity of Faithfulness*, edited by William P. Brown, 291–300. Louisville: Westminster John Knox, 2004.

Cavanaugh, William. "Killing in the Name of God." In *I Am the Lord Your God: Christian Reflections on the Ten Commandments*, edited by Carl E. Braaten and Christopher Seitz, 127–47. Grand Rapids: Eerdmans, 2005.

Debord, Guy. *Society of the Spectacle*. Translated by Ken Knabb. London: Rebel Press, 2002.

DeRouchie, Jason S. "Counting the Ten: An Investigation into the Numbering of the Decalogue." In *For Our Good Always: Studies on the Message and Influence of Deuteronomy in Honor of Daniel I. Block*, edited by Jason S. DeRouchie, Jason Gile, and Kenneth J. Turner, 93–125. Winona Lake, IN: Eisenbrauns, 2013.

Douma, J. *The Ten Commandments*. Transated by Nelson KIoosterman. Phillipsburg, NJ: P&R, 1996.

Frame, John. *Doctrine of the Christian Life*. Phillipsburg, NJ: P&R, 2008.

Greenstein, Edward L. "The Rhetoric of the Ten Commandments." In *The Decalogue in Jewish and Christian Traditions*, edited by Hennig Graf Reventlow and Yair Hoffman, 1–12. London: T&T Clark, 2012.

Griffiths, Paul. *Lying: An Augustinian Theology of Duplicity*. Eugene, OR: Wipf & Stock, 2010.

Halbertal, Moshe, and Avishai Margalit. *Idolatry*. Translated by Naomi Goldblum. Cambridge, MA: Harvard University Press, 1992.

Hamilton, Victor P. *Exodus: An Exegetical Commentary*. Grand Rapids: Baker Academic, 2011.

Hart, David Bentley. "God or Nothingness." In *I Am the Lord Your God: Christian Reflections on the Ten Commandments*, edited by Carl E. Braaten and Christopher Seitz, 55–76. Grand Rapids: Eerdmans, 2005.

Hauerwas, Stanley, and William Willimon. *The Truth about God: The Ten Commandments in Christian Life*. Nashville: Abingdon, 1999.

Havel, Vaclav. "The Power of the Powerless." history.hanover.edu/courses/excerpts/165havel.html.

Heschel, Abraham. "A Palace in Time." In *The Ten Commandments: The Reciprocity of Faithfulness*, edited by William Brown, 214–22. Louisville: Westminster John Knox, 2004.

Jenson, Robert W. "Male and Female He Created Them." In *I Am the Lord Your God: Christian Reflections on the Ten Commandments*, edited by Carl E. Braaten and Christopher Seitz, 175–88. Grand Rapids: Eerdmans, 2005.

———. *Systematic Theology*. Vol. 2, *The Works of God*. Oxford: Oxford University Press, 2001.

Jordan, James B. *Studies in Exodus: Lecture Notes*. Niceville, FL: Biblical Horizons, 1992.

Kline, Meredith. "The Two Tables of the Covenant." *Westminster* Theological Journal 22 (1960): 133–46.

Kolb, Robert, and Timothy Wengert, eds. *The Book of Concord*. Minneapolis: Fortress, 2000.

Kuntz, Paul Grimley. *The Ten Commandments in History: Mosaic Paradigms for a Well-Ordered Society*. Emory University Studies in Law and Religion. Grand Rapids: Eerdmans, 2004.

Leithart, Peter. "Chiasm of Five Words." Theopolis Institute, November 29, 2018, https://theopolisinstitute.com/leithart/chiasm-of-five-words.

———. "Counting to Ten." Theopolis Institute, February 18, 2019, https://theopolisinstitute.com/leithart/counting-to-ten.

———. "Don't Do, Don't Desire." Theopolis Institute, January 7, 2019, https://theopolisinstitute.com/leithart/dont-do-dont-desire.

———. "False Answer." Theopolis Institute, December 7, 2018, https://theopolisinstitute.com/leithart/false-answer.

Long, Stephen. "John Wesley." In *The Decalogue through the Centuries: From the Hebrew Scriptures to Benedict XVI*, edited by Jeffrey Greenman and Timothy Larsen, 169–80. Louisville: Westminster John Knox, 2012.

Lull, Ramon. *De proverbiis moralibus, tertia pars caput VIII–Caput XVII, tome II*. In *Opera omnia* 42. Mainz, 1721. Reprint, Frankfurt am Main: Minerva, 1965.

Miller, Patrick. *The Ten Commandments*. Interpretation: Resources for the Use of Scripture in the Church. Louisville: Westminster John Knox, 2009.

Mount, Ferdinand. *Full Circle: How the Classical World Came Back to Us*. New York: Simon & Schuster, 2010.

Nielsen, Eduard. *The Ten Commandments in New Perspective*. Naperville, IL: Alex R. Allenson, 1968.

North, Gary. *The Sinai Strategy: Economics and the Ten Commandments*. Tyler, TX: Institute for Christian Economics, 1986.

Pavlova, Vera. "I am in love, hence free to live." Translated by Steven Seymour. *Poetry*, January 2010, https://www.poetryfoundation.org/poetrymagazine/poems/53191/i-am-in-love-hence-free-to-live.

Powlison, David. "Idols of the Heart and 'Vanity Fair.'" *Journal of Biblical Counseling* 27, no. 3 (1995): 35–50.

Radner, Ephraim. "Taking the Lord's Name in Vain." In *I Am the Lord Your God: Christian Reflections on the Ten Commandments*, edited by Carl E. Braaten and Christopher Seitz, 77–84. Grand Rapids: Eerdmans, 2005.

Raphael Hirsch. *Horeb: A Philosophy of Jewish Laws and Observances*. Translated by Dayan Dr I. Grunfeld. New York: Soncino, 1962.

Ratzinger, Joseph. *Collected Works*. Vol. 2, *Theology of the Liturgy: The Sacramental Foundation of Christian Existence*. Edited by Michael J. Miller. Translated by John Saward et al. San Francisco: Ignatius, 2014.

Seitz, Christopher. "The Ten Commandments: Positive and Natural Law and the Covenants Old and New—Christian Use of the Decalogue and Moral Law." In *I Am the Lord Your God: Christian Reflections on the Ten Commandments*, edited by Carl E. Braaten and Christopher Seitz, 18–38. Grand Rapids: Eerdmans, 2005.

Wannenwetsch, Bernd. "You Shall Not Kill—What Does It Take? Why We Need the Other Commandments if We Are to Abstain from Killing." In *I Am the Lord Your God: Christian Reflections on the Ten Commandments*, edited by Carl E. Braaten and Christopher Seitz, 148–75. Grand Rapids: Eerdmans, 2005.

Wengert, Timothy J. "Martin Luther." In *The Decalogue through the Centuries: From the Hebrew Scriptures to Benedict XVI*, edited by Jeffrey Greenman and Timothy Larsen, 97–118. Louisville: Westminster John Knox, 2012.

SCRIPTURE INDEX

Old Testament

NAME INDEX

The Christian Essentials series is
set in TEN OLDSTYLE, designed by
Robert Slimbach in 2017. This
typeface is inspired by Italian
humanist and Japanese
calligraphy, blending
energetic formality
with fanciful
elegance.

CHRISTIAN ESSENTIALS

The Christian Essentials series passes down tradition that matters. The ancient church was founded on basic biblical teachings and practices like the Ten Commandments, baptism, the Apostles' Creed, the Lord's Supper, the Lord's Prayer, and corporate worship. These basics of the Christian life have sustained and nurtured every generation of the faithful—from the apostles to today. The books in the Christian Essentials series open up the meaning of the foundations of our faith.

For more information, visit